Christmas Music Companion Fact Book

By Dale V. Nobbman

The Chronological History of Our Most
Well-Known Traditional Christmas Hymns,
Carols, Songs And the
Writers & Composers Who Created Them

*Editors Note: Due to copyright restrictions
only the Public Domain songs have been included in this text*

ISBN 1-57424-067-6
SAN 683-8022

Cover Art: & Extra Teeth: Shawn Brown
Music Notation: George Ports
Layout: Joel Luster
Paste-up : Cindy Middlebrook
Layout and Production: Ron Middlebrook

Contents

50 All-time Favorite Traditional Christmas Songs

Dedication

This book is dedicated to all the writers and composers of our favorite Christmas hymns & carols (prior to 1960). If there were such a thing as a Christmas Music Hall of Fame then surely many of the men and women featured in this book would have to be unanimously selected for membership. Their songs have left a legacy of joy, happiness, and pleasant memories for generations of people around the world. The real life events surrounding their inspired works---read like a storybook.

The Christmas Story In Song

By Dale V. Nobbman

It Came Upon The Midnight Clear, While Shepherds Watched Their Flocks By Night (that) Angels We Have Heard On High (proclaimed) Joy To The World! (For) Away In A Manger (there is born to you this day, in the city of David, a Savior who is Christ the Lord.) (And as the) Angels From The Realms of Glory (witnessed) The First Noel, Hark! The Herald Angels (did) Sing---O Come, O Come Emmanuel, (and) O Come All Ye Faithful (to see) What Child Is This? Go Tell It On The Mountain (that it is) Sweet Little Jesus Boy (born on this) Silent Night, O Holy Night, (in the) Little Town Of Bethlehem

50 All-Time
Favorite Traditional Christmas Songs

	- Originated/Finalized -	
1. We Wish You A Merry Christmas	1600's	1600's
2. O Christmas Tree (O Tannenbaum)	1500's	1824
3. Joy To The World	1719	1839
4. The Twelve Days Of Christmas	1500's	1842
5. It Came Upon The Midnight Clear	1846	1850
6. O Come All Ye Faithful (Adeste Fidelis)	1744	1852
7. Good King Wenceslas	1853	1853
8. O Come, O Come Emmanuel	1100's	1854
9. O Holy Night	1847	1855
10. Hark! The Herald Angels Sing	1739	1857
11. We Three Kings Of Orient Are	1857	1857
12. Jingle Bells	1850	1859
13. Up On the House Top	c.1860	c.1860
14. While Shepherds Watched Their Flocks	1696	1861
15. The Holly and The Ivy	c.1700	1861
16. Silent Night	1818	1863
17. Angels From the Realms of Glory	1816	1867
18. O Little Town of Bethlehem	1868	1868
19. Here We Come A Caroling (The Wassail Song)	1600's	1871
20. God Rest Ye Merry Gentlemen	1500's	1871
21. The First Noel	1200's	1871
22. What Child Is This?	1865	1871
23. Angels We Have Heard On High	1700's	1875
24. Deck The Hall	1500's	1881
25. Away In A Manger	1885	1887
26. Jolly Old St. Nicholas	Late 1800's	L.1800's
27. Toyland	1903	1903
28. There's A Song In the Air	1872	1904
29. Go Tell It On The Mountain	1800's	1907
30. I Heard The Bells on Christmas Day	1863	1872
31. Sweet Little Jesus Boy	1932	1932
32. Santa Claus Is Coming to Town	1932	1934
33. Winter Wonderland	1934	1934
34. I Wonder As I Wander	1933	1935
35. White Christmas	1940	1942
36. I'll Be Home For Christmas	1943	1943
37. Have Yourself A Merry Little Christmas	1944	1944
38. Let It Snow, Let It Snow, Let It Snow	1945	1945
39. Here Comes Santa Claus	1946	1946
40. The Christmas Song (Chestnuts Roasting...)	1946	1946
41. Ring Christmas Bells	1947	1947
42. Blue Christmas	1948	1948
43. Rudolph the Red Nosed Reindeer	1949	1949
44. C-H-R-I-S-T-M-A-S	1949	1949
45. Silver Bells	1950	1950
46. Sleigh Ride	1948	1950
47. Frosty The Snowman	1950	1950
48. It's Beginning to Look Like Christmas	1951	1951
49. There's No Place Like Home For The Holidays	1954	1954
50. The Little Drummer Boy	1941	1958

Christmas Music Timeline

12th Century---The origins of "O Come, O Come Emmanuel" are believed to date back to this time period.

13th Century---The origins of "The First Noel" are believed to date back to this time period.

16th Century---The origins of "The Twelve Days of Christmas" are believed to date back to this time period.

16th Century---The origins of "God Rest Ye Merry Gentlemen" are believed to date back to this time period.

16th Century---The origins of "O Christmas Tree" are believed to date back to this time period.

17th Century---The origins of "We Wish You A Merry Christmas" are believed to date back to this time period.

17th Century---The origins of "Here We Come A Caroling" are believed to date back to this time period.

1580 The tune "Greensleeves" used with "What Child Is This?" was first published.

1582 The Swedish tune "Piae Cantiones" used by John Neale for "Good King Wenceslas" was composed.

1592 The original tune used with "While Shepherds Watched Their Flocks" was written by Thomas Este.

1620 "Greensleeves" was brought to America by the Pilgrims.

1642 "Greensleeves" was first published in America.

1652 Birth of Nahum Tate, author of "While Shepherds Watched Their Flocks", in Dublin, Ireland.

1674 Birth of Isaac Watts, author of "Joy To The World" in Southampton, England.

1685 Birth of George Frederick Handel, composer of "While Shepherds Watched Their Flocks" in Halle, Germany.

1696 Nahum Tate wrote the words to "While Shepherds Watched Their Flocks".

1700 The words to "While Shepherds Watched Their Flocks" were first published.

1700 "The Holly and The Ivy" made its first appearance around this time in an English "broadside".

1707 Birth of Charles Wesley, author of "Hark! The Herald Angels Sing" in Epworth, Lincolnshire, England.

1708 "While Shepherds Watched Their Flocks" was the only Christmas hymn sanctioned by the Church of England for use in worship services.

1711 Birth of John Francis Wade, author & composer of "Adeste Fideles" in England.

1715 Death of Nahum Tate (While Shepherds Watched Their Flocks) in Southwark, London, England

1719 Isaac Watts wrote the words to "Joy To The World" in his "Psalms of David".

1728 George Frederick Handel composed the music used later for "While Shepherds Watched Their Flocks".

1739 Charles Wesley wrote the original words to "Hark! The Herald Angels Sing" in his "Hymns & Sacred Poems".

1741 George Frederick Handel wrote "The Messiah" oratorio.

1742 George Frederick Handel is reputed to have composed the music used for "Joy To The World".

1744 John Francis Wade wrote the Latin words to "Adeste Fideles".

1748 Death of Isaac Watts (Joy To The World) in Abney Park, England, near London.

1751 John Francis Wade composed the music to "Adeste Fideles", and published the hymn in his "Cantus Diversi".

1753 George Whitefield revised Charles Wesleys words to "Hark! The Herald Angels Sing" in his "Collection of 1753".

1759 Death of George Frederick Handel (While Shepherds Watched Their Flocks) in London, England.

1770 "God Rest Ye Merry Gentlemen" first appeared in written form in the "Roxburghe Ballads".

1771 Birth of James Montgomery, author of "Angels From The Realms of Glory", in Irvine, Ayrshire, Scotland.

1780 The original words to "The Twelve Days of Christmas" were first published.

1782 The modern musical arrangement of "O Come All Ye Faithful" was published by Samuel Webbe.

1784 The Welsh version of "Deck The Halls" was published.

1786 Death of John Francis Wade (Adeste Fideles) in Douay, France.

1787 Birth of Franz Gruber, composer of "Silent Night" in Unterweizburg, Austria.

1788 Death of Charles Wesley (Hark! The Herald Angels Sing) in London, England.

1792 Birth of Joseph Mohr, author of "Silent Night", in Salzburg, Austria.

1792 Birth of Lowell Mason, arranger of "Joy To The World", in Medfield, Massachusetts.

1799 The melody to "O Christmas Tree" was first published.

1800 Birth of Ernst Gebhard Anschutz, author of the second and third verses of "O Christmas Tree" in Germany.

1802 Birth of Frederick Oakeley, English translator of "O Come All Ye Faithful" in Shrewsbury, England.

1803 Birth of Adolphe Adam, composer of "O Holy Night", in Paris, France.

1807 Birth of Henry W. Longfellow, author of "I Heard The Bells On Christmas Day", in Portland, Maine.

1808 Birth of Placide Cappeau de Roquemaure, author of "O Holy Night" in Roquemaure, France.

1809 Birth of Felix Mendelssohn, composer of the music used for "Hark! The Herald Angels Sing" in Hamburg, Germany.

1810 Birth of Edmund Sears, author of "It Came Upon The Midnight Clear", in Sandisfield, Massachusetts.

1811 Birth of Thomas Helmore, adapted the music for "O Come, O Come Emmanuel", in Kidderminster, England.

1813 Birth of Henry Smart, composer of "Angels From The Realms of Glory" in London, England.

1813 Birth of John Sullivan Dwight, English translator of "O Holy Night" in Boston, Massachusetts.

1816 James Montgomery wrote the words to "Angels From The Realms of Glory".

1816 Joseph Mohr wrote the words to "Silent Night".

1818 Franz Gruber composed the music for "Silent Night".

1818 Birth of John Neale, author and arranger of "Good King Wenceslas", in London, England.

1819 Birth of Richard Willis, composer of "It Came Upon The Midnight Clear", in Boston, Massachusetts.

1819 Birth of Josiah Holland, author of "There's A Song In The Air", in Belchertown, Massachusetts.

1820 Birth of John F. Young, English translator of "Silent Night", in Pittston, Maryland.

1820 Birth of John Hopkins, author of "We Three Kings", in Pittsburgh, Pennsylvannia.

1820 The original words for "O Christmas Tree" were published.

1822 Birth of James Pierpont, author and composer of "Jingle Bells", in Boston, Massachusetts.

1822 Clement Clarke Moore wrote "A Visit From St. Nicholas".

1823 The words to "The First Noel" were first printed.

1824 Ernst Gebhard Anschutz wrote the second and third verses for "O Christmas Tree".

1825 "Angels From The Realms of Glory" became universally popular after its publication in the "Christian Psalmist".

1827 The modern words for "God Rest Ye Merry Gentlemen" were first published.

1827 Birth of J. Baptiste Calkin, composer of "I Heard The Bells On Christmas Day", in London, England.

1828 "Silent Night" was first published in a German song collection between 1828 and 1833.

1830 Birth of Lewis Redner, composer of "O Little Town of Bethlehem" in Philadelphia, Pennsylvannia.

1830 The words to "The Holly and The Ivy" were first published.

1831 Birth of William Cummings, arranged the music for "Hark! The Herald Angels Sing", in Devonshire, England.

1833 "The First Noel" was first published with words & music.

1833 Birth of Benjamin Hanby, author and composer of "Up On The Housetop" in Rushville, Ohio.

1834 Birth of Uzziah Burnap, arranger of "It Came Upon The Midnight Clear" in Brooklyn, New York.

1835 Birth of Phillips Brooks, author of "O Little Town of Bethlehem", in Boston, Massachusetts.

1836 Lowell Mason arranged the music for "Joy To The World".

1837 Birth of William Dix, author of "What Child Is This?" in Bristol, England.

1838 "Silent Night" was first published in a German hymnal.

1839 "Silent Night" was first heard in America.

1839 Lowell Mason published his musical arrangement for "Joy To The World".

1840 Felix Mendelssohn wrote the music used for "Hark! The Herald Angels Sing".

1840 Birth of John Stainer, arranger and publisher of many Christmas carols, in London, England.

1841 "Silent Night" was first published in America.

1841 "O Come All Ye Faithful" was translated into English by Frederick Oakeley.

1841 Birth of James Murray, publisher of "Away In A Manger", in Ballard-Vale, Massachusetts.

1842 The modern version of "The Twelve Days Of Christmas" was published in England.

1843 "God Rest Ye Merry Gentlemen" was used in "A Christmas Carol" by Charles Dickens.

1846 Edmund Sears wrote the words to "It Came Upon The Midnight Clear".

1846 The current melody for "God Rest Ye Merry Gentlemen" was first published.

1847 Placide Cappeau de Roquemaure wrote the words to "O Holy Night".

1847 Adolphe Adam composed the music for "O Holy Night".

1847 Death of Felix Mendelssohn (Hark! The Herald Angels Sing) in Leipzig, Germany.

1848 Death of Joseph Mohr (Silent Night) in Wagrein, Austria.

1849 The words to "It Came Upon The Midnight Clear" were first published.

1850 Richard Willis composed the music for "It Came Upon The Midnight Clear".

1850 "Here We Come A Caroling" was first printed on an English "broadside".

1850 James Pierpont wrote "Jingle Bells".

1851 Birth of John McFarland, he added the third verse to "Away In A Manger", in Mt. Vernon, Indiana.

1851 John Neale translated "O Come, O Come Emmanuel" into English.

1852 Frederick Oakeley made his final English translation of the title to "O Come All Ye Faithful".

1853 John Neale wrote the words to "Good King Wenceslas".

1853 John Neale made his final English translation of "O Come, O Come Emmanuel".
1854 Thomas Helmore adapted the music for "O Come, O Come Emmanuel".
1854 Mohr and Gruber were finally identified as the author and composer of "Silent Night".
1854 Death of James Montgomery (Angels From The Realms Of Glory) in Sheffield, York, England.
1855 William Cummings arranged the music for "Hark! The Herald Angels Sing".
1855 "Angels We Have Heard On High" was first published.
1855 "O Holy Night" was translated into English by John Dwight.
1856 Death of Adolphe Adam (O Holy Night) in Paris, France.
1857 John Hopkins wrote the words to "We Three Kings".
1857 James Pierpont published "Jingle Bells" under the title "The One Horse Open Sleigh".
1857 William Cummings adaptation of "Hark! The Herald Angels Sing" was first published by Richard Chope.
1859 "Jingle Bells" was first published under this title.
1859 Birth of Victor Herbert, composer of "Toyland", in Dublin, Ireland.
1861 "The Holly and The Ivy" was first published by Joshua Sylvester.
1861 Death of Ernst Gebhard Anschutz (O Christmas Tree).
1861 Richard Willis adapted the music for "While Shepherds Watched Their Flocks".
1861 Birth of Karl Harrington, composer of "There's A Song In The Air", in Somersworth, New Hampshire.
1862 "We Three Kings" was first published.
1862 "Angels We Have Heard On High" was first translated into English.
1863 Death of Franz Gruber (Silent Night) in Hallein, Germany.
1863 "Silent Night" was translated into English.
1863 Henry W. Longfellow wrote the words to "I Heard The Bells On Christmas Day".
1865 William Dix wrote the verses to "What Child Is This?".
1866 Death of John Neale (Good King Wenceslas) in East Grimstead, England.
1867 Death of Benjamin Hanby (Up On The Housetop) in Chicago, Illinois.
1867 Henry Smart composed the music for "Angels From The Realms of Glory".
1867 "I Heard The Bells On Christmas Day" was first published under the name "Christmas Bells".
1868 "O Little Town of Bethlehem" was written and composed.
1868 The modern text of "Here We Come A Caroling" was published in "Songs of the Nativity" by W.H. Husk.
1870 Birth of Glen MacDonough, author of "Toyland", in Brooklyn, New York.
1871 "Silent Night" was first published in an American hymnal.
1871 John Stainer published the modern version of "The First Noel" in his "Christmas Carols New and Old".
1871 "We Three Kings" gained popularity by its inclusion in John Stainer's collection "Christmas Carols New and Old".
1871 John Stainer arranged and published "God Rest Ye Merry Gentlemen".
1871 John Stainer arranged the tune for "Here We Come Caroling" and published it in his "Christmas Carols New and Old".
1871 John Stainer arranged the tune for "What Child Is This?" and published it in his "Christmas Carols New and Old".
1872 Birth of John Work, author of modern verses to "Go Tell It On The Mountain", in Nashville, Tennessee.
1872 Death of Lowell Mason (Joy To The World) in Orange, New Jersey.
1872 J. Baptiste Calkin composed the music for "I Heard The Bells On Christmas Day".
1872 Josiah Holland wrote and published the words to "There's A Song In The Air".
1874 "O Little Town of Bethlehem" was first published.
1875 The modern version of "Angels We Have Heard On High" was published by Richard Chope.
1876 Death of Edmund Sears (It Came Upon The Midnight Clear) in Weston, Massachusetts.
1877 Birth of Mykola Leontovych, composer of "Ring Christmas Bells" in Monastyrak, in the Podilla Region, Ukraine.
1877 Death of Placide Cappeau de Roquemaure (O Holy Night).
1879 Death of Henry Smart (Angels From The Realms of Glory) in London, England.
1879 "Go Tell It On The Mountain" was first popularized by the Fisk Jubilee Singers.
1880 Death of Frederick Oakeley (O Come All Ye Faithful) in Islington, London, England.
1880 Birth of Frederick Work, composer of "Go Tell It On The Mountain", in Nashville, Tennessee.
1881 The words to "Deck The Halls" were first printed.
1881 Death of Josiah Holland (There's A Song In The Air) in New York City, New York.
1882 Death of Henry W. Longfellow (I Heard The Bells On Christmas Day) in Cambridge, Massachusetts.
1885 Death of John F. Young (Silent Night) in Florida.

1885 The original verses of "Away In A Manger" were first printed as a poem in Philadelphia.

1887 James Murray adapted and published "Away In A Manger".

1887 John F. Young's English translation of "Silent Night" was officially attributed to him.

1888 Birth of Irving Berlin, author and composer of "White Christmas" in Mogilev, Tyumen, Russia.

1888 Birth of Haven Gillespie, co-author of "Santa Claus Is Coming To Town", in Covington, Kentucky.

1890 Death of Thomas Helmore (O Come, O Come Emmanuel) in London, England.

1891 Death of John Hopkins Jr. (We Three Kings) in Hudson, New York.

1892 "O Little Town of Bethlehem" gains popularity by its inclusion in the Episcopal Church hymnal.

1892 The third stanza words for "Away In A Manger" were first printed.

1892 Birth of John Jacob Niles, author/composer of "I Wonder As I Wander", in Louisville, Kentucky.

1892 Birth of Katherine Davis, author of "The Little Drummer Boy", in St. Joseph, Missouri.

1893 Death of Phillips Brooks (O Little Town of Bethlehem) in Boston, Massachusetts.

1893 Death of James Pierpont (Jingle Bells) in Winter Haven, Florida.

1893 Death of John S. Dwight (O Holy Night) in Boston, Massachusetts.

1897 Birth of John F. Coots, co-author of "Santa Claus Is Coming to Town", in Brooklyn, New York.

1897 Birth of Felix Bernard, composer of "Winter Wonderland", in Brooklyn, New York.

1898 Birth of Robert MacGimsey, author/composer of "Sweet Little Jesus Boy", in Pineville, Louisianna.

1898 Death of William Dix (What Child Is This?) at Cheddar in Somerset, England.

1900 Death of Richard Willis (It Came Upon The Midnight Clear) in Detroit, Michigan.

1900 Death of Uzziah Burnap (It Came Upon The Midnight Clear) in Brooklyn, New York.

1900 Birth of Kim Gannon, author of "I'll Be Home For Christmas", in Brooklyn, New York.

1900 Birth of Mitchell Parish, author of "Sleigh Ride", in Shreveport, Louisianna.

1901 Death of John Stainer (Christmas Carols New and Old) in Verona, England.

1901 Birth of Richard Smith, author of "Winter Wonderland", in Honesdale, Pennsylvannia.

1902 Birth of Meredith Willson, author/composer of "It's Beginning To Look Like Christmas", in Mason City, Iowa.

1903 Glen MacDonough wrote the words to "Toyland".

1903 Victor Herbert composed the music for "Toyland".

1903 Birth of Jay Johnson, co-author/composer of "Blue Christmas", in Ellis, Kansas.

1904 Karl Harrington composed the music for "There's A Song In The Air".

1904 John McFarland added the third verse to "Away In A Manger" between 1904 and 1908.

1905 Death of James Murray (Away In A Manger) in Cincinnati, Ohio.

1905 Death of J. Baptiste Calkin (I Heard The Bells On Christmas Day) in Hornsey Rise Gardens, England.

1905 "There's A Song In The Air" was first published in the Methodist Hymnal.

1905 Birth of Jule Styne, composer of "Let It Snow, Let It Snow, Let It Snow", in London, England.

1906 Birth of Billy Hayes, co-author/composer of "Blue Christmas", in New York, New York.

1906 Birth of Walter Rollins, co-author of "Frosty The Snowman", in Scottdale, Pennsylvannia.

1906 Birth of Al Stillman, author of "There's No Place Like Home For The Holidays", in New York, New York.

1907 "Go Tell It On The Mountain" was published in "Folk Songs of the American Negro" by the Work brothers.

1907 Birth of Gene Autry, author of "Here Comes Santa Claus", in Tioga, Texas.

1907 Birth of Steve Edward Nelson, co-author of "Frosty The Snowman", in New York, New York.

1908 Death of Lewis Redner (O Little Town of Bethlehem) in Atlantic City, New Jersey.

1908 Birth of Leroy Anderson, composer of "Sleigh Ride", Cambridge, Massachusetts.

1909 Birth of Oakley Haldeman, composer of "Here Comes Santa Claus" in Alhambra, California.

1909 Birth of Johnny Marks, author/composer of "Rudolph The Red Nosed Reindeer", in Mt. Vernon, New York.

1910 The popularity of "It Came Upon The Midnight Clear" was advanced by its publication in "Christmas Carols & Hymns for School & Choir".

1911 Birth of Walter Kent, composer of "I'll Be Home For Christmas", in Manhattan, New York.

1911 Birth of Harry Simeone, co-arranger of "The Little Drummer Boy", in Newark, New Jersey.

1912 Birth of Henry Onorati, co-arranger of "The Little Drummer Boy", in Revere, Massachusetts.

1913 Birth of Sammy Cahn, author of "Let It Snow, Let It Snow, Let It Snow", in New York, New York.

1913 Death of John McFarland (Away In A Manger) in Maplewood, New Jersey.

1914 Birth of Hugh Martin, co-author of "Have Yourself A Merry Little Christmas", in Birmingham, Alabama.

1914 Birth of Ralph Blane, co-author of "Have Yourself A Merry Little Christmas", in Broken Arrow, Oklahoma.

1915 Death of William Cummings (Hark! The Herald Angels Sing) in Sidbury, Devonshire, England.

1915 Birth of Ray Evans, co-author/composer of "Silver Bells", in Salamanca, New York.

1915 Birth of Jay Livingston, co-author/composer of "Silver Bells", in Mc Donald, Pennsylvannia.

1915 Birth of Jenny Carson, co-author of "C-H-R-I-S-T-M-A-S", in Decatur, Illinois.

1916 Mykola Leontovych composed the music used for "Ring Christmas Bells".

1918 Birth of Eddy Arnold, co-author of "C-H-R-I-S-T-M-A-S" in Henderson, Tennessee.

1921 Death of Mykola Leontovych (Ring Christmas Bells) near Tulchin, in the Podilia Region, Ukraine.

1922 Birth of Robert Wells, author of "The Christmas Song" in Raymond, Washington.

1924 Death of Glen MacDonough (Toyland) in Stamford, Conn.

1924 Death of Victor Herbert (Toyland) in New York, New York.

1925 Birth of Mel Torme, composer of "The Christmas Song" (Chestnuts Roasting On An Open Fire), in Chicago, Ill.

1925 Death of John Work (Go Tell It On The Mountain) in Nashville, Tennessee.

1927 Birth of Robert Allen, composer of "There's No Place Like Home For The Holidays", in Troy, New York.

1932 Robert MacGimsey wrote & composed "Sweet Little Jesus Boy"

1932 Coots and Gillespie wrote and composed "Santa Claus Is Coming To Town".

1933 John Jacob Niles wrote and composed "I Wonder As I Wander".

1934 "Santa Claus Is Coming To Town" debuted on the Eddie Cantor radio show.

1934 Richard Smith wrote the words to "Winter Wonderland".

1934 Felix Bernard composed the music for "Winter Wonderland".

1935 Death of Richard Smith (Winter Wonderland) in New York, New York.

1935 "I Wonder As I Wander" was first published in "Ten Christmas Carols".

1936 Peter Wilhousky wrote the words to "Carol of the Bells".

1940 Irving Berlin wrote and composed "White Christmas".

1941 Katherine Davis wrote the words to "The Little Drummer Boy".

1942 "White Christmas" made its debut in the film "Holiday Inn".

1942 Death of Frederick Work (Go Tell It On The Mountain) in Bordentown, New Jersey.

1943 Kim Gannon wrote the words to "I'll Be Home For Christmas".

1943 Walter Kent composed the music for "I'll Be Home For Christmas".

1943 Bing Crosby recorded "I'll Be Home For Christmas".

1944 Hugh Martin and Ralph Blane wrote "Have Yourself A Merry Little Christmas".

1944 "Have Yourself A Merry Little Christmas" debuted in the Judy Garland film "Meet Me In St.Louis".

1944 Death of Felix Bernard (Winter Wonderland) in Hollywood, California.

1945 Sammy Cahn wrote the words to "Let It Snow, Let It Snow, Let It Snow".

1945 Jule Styne composed the music for "Let It Snow, Let It Snow, Let It Snow".

1946 "Let It Snow, Let It Snow, Let It Snow" was recorded by Vaughn Monroe.

1946 Gene Autry wrote the words to "Here Comes Santa Claus".

1946 Oakley Haldeman composed the music for "Here Comes Santa Claus".

1946 Mel Torme and Robert Wells co-authored "The Christmas Song" (Chestnuts Roasting On An Open Fire).

1947 M.L. Hohman wrote the words and published "Ring Christmas Bells".

1947 "Here Comes Santa Claus" became popular.

1948 Billy Hayes and Jay Johnson co-authored "Blue Christmas".

1948 Leroy Anderson composed the music for "Sleigh Ride".

1949 Johnny Marks wrote and composed "Rudolph The Red Nosed Reindeer".

1949 "Rudolph The Red Nosed Reindeer" debuted at Madison Square Garden by Gene Autry.

1949 Eddy Arnold and Jenny Carson co-authored "C-H-R-I-S-T-M-A-S".

1950 "Silver Bells" was written, composed, and then debuted in the film "The Lemon Drop Kid" in 1951.

1950 "Winter Wonderland" became a big hit for the Andrew Sisters.

1950 Mitchell Parish wrote the words for "Sleigh Ride".

1950 Steve Nelson and Walter Rollins co-authored "Frosty The Snowman".

1950 "Frosty The Snowman" was recorded by Gene Autry.

1951 Meredith Willson wrote and composed "It's Beginning To Look Like Christmas".

1953 Death of Karl Harrington (There's A Song In The Air) in Middletown, Conn.

1954 Al Stillman and Robert Allen co-authored/composed "There's No Place Like Home For The Holidays".

1958 Harry Simeone and Henry Onorati re-titled Katherine Davis' song "Carol of the Drums" to "The Little Drummer Boy".
1973 Death of Walter Rollins (Frosty The Snowman) in Cincinnati, Ohio.
1974 Death of Kim Gannon (I'll Be Home For Christmas) in Delray Beach, Florida.
1975 Death of Haven Gillespie (Santa Claus Is Coming To Town) in Las Vegas, Nevada.
1975 Death of Leroy Anderson (Sleigh Ride) in Woodbury, Connecticut.
1978 Death of Jenny Carson (C-H-R-I-S-T-M-A-S) in California.
1979 Death of Robert MacGimsey (Sweet Little Jesus Boy) in Phoenix, Arizona.
1979 Death of Al Stillman (There's No Place Like Home For The Holidays) in New York, New York.
1980 Death of John J. Niles (I Wonder As I Wander) in Lexington, Kentucky.
1980 Death of Katherine Davis (The Little Drummer Boy) in Concord, Massachusetts.
1981 Death of Steve Edward Nelson (Frosty The Snowman).
1984 Death of Meredith Willson (It's Beginning To Look Like Christmas) in Santa Monica, California.
1985 Death of Johnny Marks (Rudolph The Red Nosed Reindeer) in New York, New York.
1985 Death of John F. Coots (Santa Claus Is Coming To Town).
1986 Death of Oakley Haldeman (Here Comes Santa Claus).
1986 Death of Jay W. Johnson (Blue Christmas).
1989 Death of Irving Berlin (White Christmas) in New York, New York.
1993 Death of Sammy Cahn (Let It Snow, Let It Snow, Let It Snow) in Los Angeles, California.
1993 Death of Mitchell Parish (Sleigh Ride) in New York, New York.
1993 Death of Henry Onorati (The Little Drummer Boy).
1994 Death of Jule Styne (Let It Snow, Let It Snow, Let It Snow) in New York, New York.
1994 Death of Walter Kent (I'll Be Home For Christmas) In Los Angeles, California.
1995 Death of Ralph Blane (Have Yourself A Merry Little Christmas) in Broken Arrow, Oklahoma.
1998 Death of Gene Autry (Here Comes Santa Claus) in Los Angeles, California.
1999 Death of Mel Torme (The Christmas Song) in Los Angeles, California.

The Origin of Christmas Hymns and Carols

Christmas is a time of religious contemplation, gift-giving, joy, the hope for peace on earth, and carols & hymns that reflect all these activities and desires. Our traditional Christmas carols have developed over a period of many centuries from many forms and sources. Carols were at one time "danced to" as well as sung. Most of them were originally sung in unison, unaccompanied, with the present harmonizations added much later. Some are carry-overs from Pagan times, with changes in lyrics by their Christian adaptors. Others originated as hymns, and many as poems to which melodies were later composed. Some Christmas hymns and carols have been written, composed, and completed within a days time, others have taken centuries to see the words, translations, titles, compositions, and adaptations come together into the songs we are familiar with today. Some traditional Christmas songs with famous titles have fallen from modern popularity, such as, "The Coventry Carol", "The Boar's Head Carol", "Masters In This Hall", "Lo, How A Rose E'er Blooming", and "Bring A Torch, Jeannette, Isabella". Only a handful of songs have withstood the test of time.

Hymns are defined as "songs of praise to God", and "songs of joy". Their metrical composition is adapted for singing in a religious service. Carols are traditional "songs of joyful character". A further brief look at the history of our Christmas carols and hymns continues as follows:

Music for Christmastime began with the "litanies" (musical prayers) of the Christian Church. Until the 13th century only church officials were encouraged to sing at church services. Then in the early 1200's, St. Francis of Assisi encouraged others to sing hymns and carols. As a result, St. Francis is known as the "Father of Caroling". The word "carol" is derived from the word "carola" which means a ring dance. Carols have long been considered an early form of sacred folk music, dating from the Middle Ages. During this period the carols seem to have been an essential part of the early mystery and miracle plays which were widely used by the medieval church for teaching its religious dogmas. The carols were sung during these plays for entertainment between the various scenes. After the plays, the carolers strolled down the street, still singing. This is how the practice of "street caroling" came about. Then, in 1644, the English Puritan parliament abolished the celebration of Christmas and all other "worldly festivals", because the celebrations had become too rowdy and were believed to have lost the inner and spiritual meaning of Christmas. Christmas celebrations in America were banned for a time by the Puritans in Massachusetts from 1659 to 1681. As a result, during the remainder of the 17th century and well into the 18th century, there was a scarcity of these folk-like carol hymns in England and America. Charles Dicken's "A Christmas Carol", in 1843, helped revitalize the celebration of Christmas in England, and thus, a renewed interest in singing carols and hymns.

Today, when it rolls around to December, it is customary to sing the hymns that honor the birth of Jesus Christ, and to sing along with the secular carols, which often focus on Santa Claus. The birth of Jesus is placed in history about 5 B.C., however, the first mention of the observance of Christmas on December 25th is in the year 325 A.D. Egyptian historian, Julius Sextus Africanus, is credited with establishing the day for Jesus' birth on that date we have observed ever since, but there are as many as four Pagan, Roman, and Jewish customs, festivals, ceremonies, and celebrations connected to the 25th of December that may have influenced the choice of December 25th as the date to celebrate Jesus' birth. Using this date to clebrate Christmas was a way for Christians to 'counter' the long established non-Christian festivities prevalent at the time. Late in the fourth century, St. Chrysostom, Bishop of Constantinople, wrote that "on this day (the 25th) also the Brithday of Christ was lately fixed at Rome in order that while the heathen were busy with their profane ceremonies, the Christians might perform their sacred rites undisturbed". The Romans began observing Christmas around 350 A.D. The Pope at Jerusalem and most other Christians accepted the date about a century later in 440 A.D. (In 354 A.D., Bishop Liberius of Rome actually "ordered" the people to celebrate Christmas on December 25th). Also, in the year 325 A.D., a bishop of Myra, from Asia Minor, Saint Nicholas, attended the Church Council of Nicea. He was famous for his generosity, and people came to believe that any surprise gift came from him. The people of The Netherlands chose him as the patron saint of children and his fame gradually spread. The Dutch form of Saint Nicholas is "Sinterklaas", from which we get the contemporary "Santa Claus". Clement Clarke Moore gave us our modern description of "Santa Claus" in his poem "A Visit from St. Nicholas" in 1822.

Christmas Music Overview Through The Years

In the years between 1644 and 1691, when the Puritans were trying to ban the celebration of Christmas in England, as well as, in the Massachusetts colony in America, the future of our favorite Christmas music was about to be secured for all the centuries to follow, with the births of Nahum Tate (1652), Isaac Watts (1674), and George Frederick Handel (1685). They were talented, inspired, and influential men in the world of music, and "pioneers" in the creation of enduring Christmas songs. During this period of time, when the American colonies were establishing themselves in the New World, English folk carols originating in the streets of England included, "We Wish You A Merry Christmas" and "Here We Come A Caroling". The only other early carols (still popular today) being sung then in their original forms were "O Come, O Come Emmanuel", "The First Noel", "The Twelve Days of Christmas", "God Rest Ye Merry Gentlemen", and "O Christmas Tree".

The early 1700's proved to be a turning point for the beginning of a new era in the popularity of Christmas music. In 1700, the words to "While Shepherds Watched Their Flocks", by Nahum Tate, were first published. About this same time, "The Holly and The Ivy" made its first appearance in an English broadside. The year 1707 was pivotal for Christian music in general, with the birth of Charles Wesley, author of over 6,500 hymns, and with the publication of "Hymns and Spiritual Songs", by Isaac Watts, the "Father of Modern English Hymnody". Watts' peers at the time were, Daniel Defoe in literature, Isaac Newton in science, Johann Sebastian Bach and George F. Handel in music. In 1708, "While Shepherds Watched Their Flocks" was the only Christmas hymn sanctioned by the Church of England for use in worship services. At this point, Christmas music still had a very long way to go in establishing itself as a form of influential music with "lasting power".

The world noted the passing of Nahum Tate in 1715, the same year that Isaac Watts published "Divine Songs for Children". Watts followed this collection of songs with the publication of "Psalms of David" in 1719, which included his words for "Joy To The World". Daniel Defoe published "Robinson Crusoe" that year, and George F. Handel was selected to become the director of the Royal Academy of Music in London. Handel actively wrote opera music through the 1720's, and in 1728, he composed the music to be used later with "While Shepherds Watched Their Flocks". Ten years passed before anything of further importance occurred regarding the advancement of Christmas music. During this time, Handel and Bach continued to produce their "classical" music.

In 1738, John and Charles Wesley experienced their life changing evangelical conversion. The following year in 1739, Charles Wesley celebrated the one year anniversary of his conversion by writing the original words to "Hark! The Herald Angels Sing". Two years later, Handel wrote his "The Messiah" oratorio, completed in the short span of 23 days. Handel is reputed to have composed the music for "Joy To The World" in 1742, however, this fact has never been confirmed as true. In 1744, France declared war on

England. It so happened that a British exile living in France at the time, John Francis Wade, wrote the Latin words to "Adeste Fideles". French and British hostilities continued into the 1750's, and actually expanded to the New World where the two countries competed for American land. John Francis Wade composed the music for "Adeste Fideles" and published the hymn in his "Cantus Diversi" collection of 1751. The only other notable event regarding Christmas music to take place in the 1750's, was when revivalist, George Whitefield, revised Charles Wesley's words for "Hark! The Herald Angels Sing" in his published "Collection of 1753", giving us the modern rendition of the words we sing today.

In 1759, the world mourned the passing of George F. Handel. He had been a creative force in music throughout the first half of the 18th century. A dry spell occurred in the advancement of Christmas music all through the 1760's, up to and beyond the American Revolution of 1776, and into the early 1780's. Bach, Wolfgang Amadeus Mozart, and Franz Joseph Hayden dominated the world of music through the 1760's and 1770's. The only thing notable in the realm of Christmas music during this period was the first written appearance of "God Rest Ye Merry Gentlemen" in the Roxburghe Ballads of 1770.

In the early 1780's, the American Revolution was officially coming to an end, and the first works by Ludwig van Beethoven were published. The original words to "The Twelve Days Of Christmas" were first published in 1780, and in 1782, the modern musical arrangement for "O Come All Ye Faithful" was published by Samuel Webbe. The latter 1780's and early 1790's were dominated by the music of Mozart, Haydn, and Beethoven. During this same period, Christmas music, and other Christian music in general, lost the talents of Charles Wesley and John Francis Wade, but saw the births of Lowell Mason, Franz Gruber, and Joseph Mohr. The end of the 18th century witnessed the rise of Napoleon to power in Europe. The century ended with the death of George Washington in 1799, along with the publication of the melody used for "O Christmas Tree" that same year.

The 19th century saw an increased interest in the creation of Christmas music. In the first two decades of the 1800's, Beethoven and Franz Schubert were composing symphonies, the United States was defeating the British in the War of 1812, and Europe was ridding itself of Napoleon. Between 1800 and 1820, the future of Christmas music was bright with the births of Frederick Oakeley, Adolphe Adam, Henry Wadsworth Longfellow, Placide Cappeau de Roquemaure, Felix Mendelssohn, Edmund Sears, Thomas Helmore, Henry Smart, John S. Dwight, John Mason Neale, Richard Willis, Josiah Holland, John F. Young, and John Hopkins Jr. Towards the end of this important twenty year period, James Montgomery wrote the words to "Angels From The Realms Of Glory" in 1816. In 1818, Joseph Mohr and Franz Gruber teamed up to create the most famous of all Christmas songs, "Silent Night", on Christmas Eve of that year. The original stanza's for "O Christmas Tree" were first published in 1820.

In 1822, Clement Clarke Moore wrote "A Visit From St. Nicholas", which would influence some future secular Christmas songs. The remainder of the 1820's saw the publication of the words for "The First Noel" in 1823, the second and third verses added to "O Christmas Tree" by Ernst Anschutz in 1824, and the publication of the modern words for

"God Rest Ye Merry Gentlemen" in 1827. The next decade between 1828 and 1837 enjoyed the works of Felix Mendelssohn and Chopin. Another group of men were born during this decade who would shape the world of Christmas music through the 1850's, 1860's, and the post American Civil War years. This group included J. Baptiste Calkin, Lewis Redner, William Cummings, Benjamin Hanby, Phillips Brooks, and William Dix. In 1833, Johannes Brahms was born, and "The First Noel" was first published with words and music.

The thirty year period between 1838 and 1868 was a most productive period in the development of our favorite Christmas "hymns". During that time, a string of musical events left us with a good deal of the Christmas music legacy we are blessed with today. On one hand, this was a dark time in U.S. history, with social and political events leading up to and culminating in the American Civil War, but this same period gave us many current renditions of Christmas songs that we sing today. In 1839, "Silent Night" was first being heard and sang in the United States. That same year, Lowell Mason published his music for "Joy To The World". In 1840, Felix Mendelssohn wrote the music used for "Hark! The Herald Angels Sing", and the following year Frederick Oakeley translated "Adeste Fideles" into English. Charles Dickens used "God Rest Ye Merry Gentlemen" in his 1843 "A Christmas Carol". Three years later, Edmund Sears wrote the words to "It Came Upon The Midnight Clear". In 1847, Placide Cappeau de Roquemaure and Adolphe Adam wrote and composed "O Holy Night". The words to "It Came Upon The Midnight Clear" were first published in 1849, and Richard Willis composed the music for this hymn the very next year of 1850. The yearly string of Christmas music developments continued in 1850 with the first printing of the words to "Here We Come A Caroling", in England. In 1851, John Mason Neale translated "O Come, O Come Emmanuel" into English, and Frederick Oakeley made his final English translation of "O Come All Ye Faithful" in 1852. John Mason Neale made his final English translation of " O Come, O Come Emmanuel" in 1853, and that same year, Neale wrote the words to "Good King Wenceslas". In 1854, Thomas Helmore adapted the music of his friend and co-worker, Neale, and left us with the Christmas hymn "O Come, O Come Emmanuel", as we know it today. Also, in 1854, a group of musical researchers confirmed and proclaimed Joseph Mohr and Franz Gruber as the author and composer of "Silent Night". Up till then, the popularity of "Silent Night" had grown in Europe and America, without the benefit of knowing who had authored the hymn. In the following year of 1855, William Cummings arranged the music for "Hark! The Herald Angels Sing". It was this same year that "Angels We Have Heard On High" was first published, and John Sullivan Dwight translated "O Holy Night" into English. In 1857, while John Hopkins Jr. was writing and composing "We Three Kings", James Pierpont was publishing his new song "Jingle Bells". Also, that year, William Cummings' adaptation of "Hark! The Herald Angels Sing" was first published.

During the American Civil War, "The Holly and The Ivy" was first published, in 1861. and that same year, Richard Willis made his second contribution to Christmas music by adapting the music for "While Shepherds Watched Their Flocks". The next year, "We Three Kings" was first published, and "Angels We Have Heard On High" was translated into English. In 1863, "Silent Night" was finally translated into the English words we use today by John Freeman Young. The famous poet, Henry Wadsworth Longfellow, wrote the words to "I Heard The Bells On Christmas Day" in 1863. William Dix wrote the verses used for "What Child Is This?" in 1865. In the post Civil War years, the creation of Christmas music began to ebb once again. A couple of exceptions during this period were that Henry Smart composed the music for "Angels From The Realms Of Glory" in 1867, and Phillips Brooks and Lewis Redner wrote and composed "O Little Town Of Bethlehem" in 1868. That same year the modern text we use for "Here We Come A Caroling" was published.

In the 1870's, Brahms and Tchaikovsky were the masters of the classical music world. Sir John Stainer advanced the popularity of "The First Noel", "We Three Kings", "God Rest Ye Merry Gentlemen", "Here We Come A Caroling", and "What Child Is This?" by including them in his 1871 publication "Christmas Carols New and Old". In 1872, J. Baptiste Calkin composed the music for "I Heard The Bells On Christmas Day", and Josiah Holland wrote the words for "There's A Song In The Air". "O Little Town of Bethlehem" was first published in 1874, and the modern version of "Angels We Have Heard On High" was published in 1875. In 1879, "Go Tell It On The Mountain" was being popularized by the Fisk Jubilee Singers.

In 1881, the modern words to "Deck The Halls" were first printed. The original verses of "Away In A Manger" were first printed in 1885. James Murray adapted the music to those words and published "Away In A Manger" in 1887. In the late 1800's, at the same time that the creation of 19th century Christmas music was winding down, important music makers of the 20th century were being born. This group included Irving Berlin, Haven Gillespie, John Niles, Katherine Davis, John Coots, and Felix Bernard. At the same time, during the last two decades of the 19th century, the world observed the passing of Thomas Helmore, John Hopkins Jr., Phillips Brooks, James Pierpont, John Dwight, and William Dix.

The 20th century began about the same, with the birth and passing of Christmas music makers. During the first three decades of the 20th century, and up to the Great Depression years of the 1930's, there was an obvious absence of newly created, quality Christmas songs. The exceptions during this period were "Toyland", "There's A Song In The Air", and "Go Tell It On The Mountain".

The most recent era to give us lasting traditional Christmas songs stretched from 1932 to 1958. The depression years gave us "Sweet Little Jesus Boy", "Santa Claus Is Coming To Town", "Winter Wonderland", and "I Wonder As I Wander". The war years of World War II gave us "White Christmas", "I'll Be Home For Christmas", "Have Yourself A Merry Little Christmas", and "Let It Snow, Let It Snow, Let It Snow". The post war and early "baby boomer" years gave us another dozen of our favorite Christmas songs which now qualify as "traditional Christmas favorites".

The creation of Christmas music continues up to the present, but that's a subject for another book. We close the "Christmas Music Companion Fact Book" with our traditional Christmas songs which have survived the toughest test of all---the test of time.

We Wish You A Merry Christmas

Author Unknown,
Traditional 17th century, English carol

We Wish You A Merry Christmas" is one of a group of English carols termed "traditional", because the authors are unknown and the origin of the music is uncertain. Dates surrounding the creation of this carol cannot be fixed and may forever remain part of our intriguing musical mysteries. It's most likely though that this carol has been passed down through the years virtually unchanged in its wording and melody, since its origin in the 17th century. It is known that this carol was sung by a municipal chorus of singers, originally called "minstrels" in medieval days, and later called "waits", in old England of the seventeenth century. They were public musicians employed to play for processions or public entertainment. Waits were especially busy at Christmastime, serenading for gratuities, and telling the Nativity story in song, and generally making the festivities of our favorite holiday even merrier. Today, this cheerful Christmas song with its wish for a merry Christmas often serves as a sort of farewell benediction from the door to door caroling groups as they conclude their singing at homes along the streets.

Historical Setting For "We Wish You A Merry Christmas":

The Stuart dynasty thrived in England during the 17th century.

Oliver Cromwell was a leading figure in England during the 17th century.

The English settlement of Jamestown was established in America in the 17th century.

We Wish You a Merry Christmas

O Christmas Tree

1st stanza Author Unknown
Traditional German carol from the 16th century
2nd & 3rd stanzas by: Ernst Gebhard Anschutz (1800-1861) in 1824
Original German title: "O Tannenbaum"

The evergreen has been used as a symbol of eternal life since ancient days, beginning with the Egyptians, Chinese and Hebrews. The Romans adorned trees with decorations and gifts during their winter festival called Saturnalia. During the Barbarian Invasions of the Roman Empire, the Goths adopted some of the Roman customs, and returned to Germany with them. During the German "Mystery Plays" of the 11th through the 15th century, the decorated tree played a big part in the "Paradise" play, about the Garden of Eden. The custom of decorating trees in our homes as part of our Christmas festivities arose in Germany, during the lifetime of Martin Luther, after church authorities in Germany suspended all mystery plays in churches. Tradition has it that Martin Luther himself may have originated the practice, following a walk through the forest on Christmas Eve, when the stars shining through the evergreen trees impressed him so much that he attempted to show his family a sight like it by cutting down an evergreen and decorating it with lighted candles.

As a Christian symbol, the evergreen tree represents the unchanging and living Christ. The tradition of the Christmas tree came to America with the Hessian (German) mercenaries who fought with the British during the American Revolutionary War. Today, the decorated tree custom is the most universal Christmas holiday decoration around the world. This is the second most famous German language Christmas song, next to "Silent Night". The melody we use today was first published in "Melodien zum Mildheimischen Liederbuche" in 1799 for a song titled "Es lebe Doch", and the original words were first published in "Weisenbuch zu den Volksliedern fur Volkschulen" by August Zarnack in Berlin in 1820, but we do not know for sure who wrote the words to the famous first verse of this song. We do know that German poet Ernst Gebhard Anschutz wrote the second and third stanzas of the song in 1824.

Historical Setting For "O Christmas Tree":

George Washington died in 1799, the year the melody for this carol was first published.

Maine became a State in 1820, when the original words to this carol were first published.

Florence Nightingale and Susan B. Anthony were born in 1820.

Portland cement was invented in 1824, when additional verses were added to "O Christmas Tree" by German poet, Ernst Anschutz.

O Christmas Tree

Moderately

(O Tannenbaum!)

O Christ - mas Tree, O Christ - mas Tree, You stand in ver - dant beau - ty! O

Christ - mas Tree, O Christ - mas Tree, You stand in ver - dant beau - ty! Your

boughs are green in sum - mer's glow, And do not fade in win - ter's snow. O

Christ - mas Tree, O Christ - mas Tree, You stand in ver - dant beau - ty!

Joy To The World

Words by: Isaac Watts (1674-1748) in 1719
Composition credited to: George Frederick Handel (1685-1759) in 1742
Arranged by: Lowell Mason (1792-1872) in 1839
Original title: "The Messiah's Coming and Kingdom"
Scripture Reference: Luke 2:1O, Psalm 98

Isaac Watts was born in Southampton, England, the oldest of nine children. He was small in stature, standing a mere five feet tall. Considered the "Father of Modern English Hymnody", he was the first Englishman to succeed in overcoming the prejudices that opposed the introduction of hymns into English public worship.

"Joy To The World" was included in Watts' well-known hymnal of 1719, "Psalms of David Imitated in the Language of the New Testament". A translation of the last five verses of Psalm 98 was used as a scripture reference for this hymn, and Watts first titled his text "The Messiah's Coming and Kingdom". In all, Isaac Watts wrote approximately 6OO hymns in his lifetime.

Watts and Handel lived in London during the same time period and evidently knew each other. Handel has been credited with composing the music for this hymn, however, there is no proof that Handel had anything to do with the composition of "Joy To The World". The actual composition credit should go to music educator Lowell Mason. It was Mason who created the confusion over the composition, by including the phrase "From George Frederick Handel", because he used a couple excerpts from Handel's "Messiah" when he set the text to music.

Lowell Mason was born in Medfield, Mass., and published more than 4O collections of sacred music, and wrote or arranged more than 1,5OO hymn tunes. His music career began in 1822 with the publication of his first hymn collection. In 1832, he founded the Boston Academy of Music for the purpose of teaching music to the masses. He went on to obtain the title "Father of American Church and Public School Music". Mason co-founded the New York Normal Institute with George F. Root and William B. Bradbury, in 1853, for the purpose of training music teachers. In 1855, he received the first ever honorary "Doctor of Music" degree in America.

Mason's rearrangement of the music to this hymn was made in 1836 and was published in 1839 (12O years after the words were written) during his time at the Academy of Music, and appeared in his "Modern Psalmist" using the adapted tune known as "Antioch".

Historical Setting For "Joy To The World":

Daniel Defoe published "Robinson Crusoe" in 1719, the same year that "Joy To The World" made its first appearance in print.

Joy to the World

3. No more let sin and sorrow grow,
   Nor thorns infest the ground;
   He comes to make His blessings flow
   Far as the curse is found,
   Far as the curse is found,
   Far as, far as the curse is found.

4. He rules the world with truth and grace,
   And makes the nations prove
   The glories of His righteousness.
   And wonders of His love,
   And wonders of His love,
   And wonders, and wonders of His love.

The Twelve Days of Christmas

Author Unknown
Traditional 16th century English carol

This carol probably dates from the 16th century, when such counting songs were very much in fashion. During the Victorian period it became a popular parlor game for kids. Dates regarding it's creation are not able to be verified, however, an early version appeared in a nursery book titled "Mirth Without Mischief" in 1780 in England, which certainly advanced the songs popularity. This is another English carol with an anonymous author and composer. J.O. Helliwell published today's modern version with the current wording of gifts in England in 1842. However, the song really did not become popular in the U.S. until the 1940's.

In the Middle Ages, religious holidays were practically the only holidays, and lord and peasant alike tried to extend such happy times as long as possible. So it is, that the Medieval English monarchs seem to have helped put the "merry" in the "Merry Christmas" greeting we use today. 16th century poet, Thomas Tusser, summed up the festive spirit with which Christmas was celebrated in the England of that day with his phrase "At Christmas, play and make good cheer, for Christmas comes but once a year". Christmas became not just one day of celebration, but twelve, extending from Christmas Day to the Epiphany, when the Wise Men arrived with their gifts for the infant Jesus. A common practice in earlier days was to exchange a gift on each of the twelve days of Christmas.

Historical Setting For "The Twelve Days of Christmas":

The world's first hymn book was published in Prague by Severin in the 16th century, about the same time this carol had its origins.

Da Vinci painted the "Mona Lisa" in the 16th century.

Martin Luther posted the "Ninety-Five Theses" in the 16th century.

Michelangelo completed the "Pieta" and "David" sculptures and painted the ceiling of the Sistine Chapel in the 16th century.

Estimated population of the American Colonies stood at 2.8 million people in 1780, when this carol made its first appearance in print.

William Walford wrote the hymn "Sweet Hour of Prayer" in 1842, the same year the modern version of this carol was published.

The Twelve Days of Christmas

Moderately

7. On the seventh day of Christmas my true love sent to me:
   Seven swans a-swimming.

8. ...Eight maids a-milking

9. ...Nine ladies dancing

10. ..Ten lords a-leaping

11. ...'Leven pipers piping

12. ...Twelve drummers drumming

27

It Came Upon The Midnight Clear

Words by: Edmund Hamilton Sears (1810-1876) in 1846
Composed by: Richard Storrs Willis (1819-1900) in 1850
Scripture Reference: Luke 2:9-14

This was the 1st American Christmas song with international appeal. In fact, it was the first Christmas song, written by an American, to achieve lasting popularity. Edmund Sears was born in Sandisfield, Massachusetts, the son of a farmer, and he became a Unitarian clergyman in 1839. He wrote this hymn while serving a Wayland, Mass. parish.

It is said that Sears wrote the words to this hymn in 1846, but that the poem stayed in his desk until his text first appeared in the December 29 issue of a Unitarian periodical "The Christian Register" in Boston, in 1849.

After his song gained popularity, the public praise he received dismayed him somewhat, because he was one who preferred to lead a quiet life in his small parish. Sears left the Wayland Parish in 1865 and became minister at the First Parish Church, Weston, Mass. until his death in 1876. The original manuscript of this hymn is preserved in the Sears Memorial Chapel, First Parish Church, Weston, Mass. Sears authored a number of deeply spiritual books during his life, and served as the editor of the "Monthly Religious Magazine" from 1859 to 1871, but he is primarily remembered for this famous Christmas hymn. He did author a lesser-known Christmas hymn in 1834, while a student at Union College in New York, titled "Calm on the Listening Ear of Night". These were the only two hymn texts he was ever known to write.

The composer, Richard Willis, was born in Boston, and became a Catholic music critic, and an editor for the New York Tribune. As a young man, Willis studied music in Europe, with, among others, Felix Mendelssohn. He published several collections of hymns during his lifetime. From his Organ Study #23 the tune titled "Carol", from 1850, would come to be used with this hymn. The tune was originally used with another hymn text, "See Israel's Gentle Shepherd Stand" in Willis' "Church Chorals and Choir Studies".

Uzziah Christopher Burnap (1834-1900) is said to have rearranged Willis' work into a hymn tune that better fit Sears poetry. Burnap was born in Brooklyn, NY and was a dry goods merchant for some time. He studied music in Paris, became a prolific composer, and was the organist for the Reformed Church of Brooklyn Heights for 37 years. The hymns 20th century popularity was advanced by its publication in "Christmas Carols and Hymns for School and Choir" in 1910.

It Came Upon the Midnight Clear

O Come All Ye Faithful

Latin words by: John Francis Wade (1711-1786) in 1744
Music by: John Francis Wade (1711-1786) in 1751
English Translation by: Frederick Oakeley (1802-1880) in 1841
Original title: "Adeste Fideles"
Scripture Reference: Luke 2:13-15

John Francis Wade was an 18th-century British exile living at the Roman Catholic center in Douay, France. An English University located there served as a shelter for religious and political refugees from England's internal strife (especially during the Jacobite rebellion of 1745).

Wade's main income came from copying and selling music, and giving music lessons. He wrote the Latin stanzas to "Adeste Fideles" in 1744, and then combined the text with music and published the hymn in 1751, in his collection of songs known as "Cantus Diversi". It proceeded to gain popularity with the Catholics in France, where it was used at the annual Benediction of the Christmas Mass.

The hymn was published again in "An Essay on the Church Plain Chant" in 1782, by Samuel Webbe, (1740-1816) an English organist and composer. In this work, the tune as we know it today was matched by Webbe with Wade's Latin text. In England, the melody of the hymn has for many generations been called "Portuguese Hymn", because the Duke of Leeds heard the hymn at the Portuguese Chapel in London, in about 1785, and incorrectly assumed it to be of Portuguese origin. The hymn has become one of the most universally popular songs of praise, having been translated into more than 119 languages.

Frederick Oakeley was born in Shrewsbury, England. He was a clergyman, and one of the Tractarian authors during the Oxford Movement in England (which advocated that certain Roman Catholic practices be restored in the Church of England). His involvement with the movement created great controversy, leading to his resignation from the Church of England in 1845. He later joined the Roman Catholic Church and was Canon of Westminster diocese from 1852 to 1880. His fame rests primarily with his translation of the popular 18th-century hymn "Adeste Fidelis" into English in 1841, for use at the Margaret Street Chapel. "Adeste Fidelis" translates in English to "Come hither, ye faithful". Oakeley changed his 1841 English title of the song from "Ye Faithful Approach Ye" to "O Come All Ye Faithful" in 1852. The completed hymn first appeared in F.H. Murray's 1852 collection, "A Hymnal For Use In The English Church", published in London.

Historical Setting For "O Come All Ye Faithful":

The King George's War began in 1744, the same year Wade wrote the Latin text to this hymn.

O Come, All Ye Faithful

Good King Wenceslas

Words by: John Mason Neale (1818-1866) in 1853
Traditional Swedish tune from 1582
Arranged by: Thomas Helmore (1811-189O) in 1853

John Mason Neale wrote this carol in 1853 as a subject for a children's song. It first appeared in "Neale's Carol's for Christmastide". The song is based on a legend about Wenceslas, the real life Duke of Bohemia, who ruled from 928 to 935 A.D. He became renowned for his kindness to his subjects, especially on Christmas day and St. Stephen's day, which is on December 26. Unfortunately, his envious younger brother murdered Wenceslas. The verses of the song by Neale form a dialogue between the King and his page about a poor peasant and how the King took mercy on him.

John Neale was born in London, England. He was the son of a minister, and followed his father into the clergy. Neale wrote more than 6O original hymns during his lifetime. Neale used a tune, which dated back to 1582 for use with his text to this song. The tune was originally used with a Swedish spring carol with a Latin text commencing "Tempus adest floridum", meaning "Spring has unwrapped her flowers". It appeared in a collection of Swedish church and school songs titled "Piae Cantiones" compiled by Theodoric Petri of Nyland, Finland (then part of Sweden). Neale received a copy of Petri's book in 1853 and wrote the words for this song specifically to the music.

Neale was a student of the liturgies and practices of the early church, and was one of the first to translate ancient Greek and Latin hymns into English. As a result, he is credited with promoting the popularity of Christmas carols. He suffered from poor health most of his life, and as the climate in England did not agree with him, he spent a great deal of time on the Island of Madeira, off the coast of Portugal. Neale served as a warden in a home for the impoverished at East Grinstead, Sussex, England, from 1846 to 1863. It was there that he founded the Anglican nursing sisterhood of St. Margaret's in 1854.

Thomas Helmore did the musical settings and harmonies for this song during the time he was serving as Precentor of St. Mark's College, in Chelsea, England, beginning in 1841.

Historical Setting For "Good King Wenceslas":

The Gregorian calender system we currently use was created by Pope Gregory XIII in 1582, the same year the music for this carol was composed.

Neale wrote this song the same year that Commodore Matthew Perry negotiated a treaty with Japan to open that country to U.S. ships, in 1853.

Millard Fillmore handed the U.S. Presidency over to Franklin Pierce in 1853.

Good King Wenceslas

Moderately

Good King Wen - ces - las looked out   On the feast of   Ste - phen,
"Hith - er, page, and stand by me,   If thou know'st it,   tell - ing,

When the snow lay 'round a - bout,   Deep, and crisp, and   e - ven;
Yon - der pea - sant, who is he?   Where and what his   dwell - ing?"

Bright - ly shone the moon that night,   Through the frost was   cru - el,
'Sire, he lives a good league hence,   Un - der - neath the   moun - tain,

When a poor man came in sight,   Gath - 'ring win - ter   fu - el.
Right a - gainst the for - est fence,   By Saint Ag - nes'   foun - tain.'

3. 'Bring me flesh, and bring me wine.
   Bring me pine-logs hither:
   Thou and I will see him dine,
   When we bear them thither.'
   Page and monarch, forth they went,
   Forth they went together;
   Through the rude wind's wild lament
   and the bitter weather.

4. 'Sire, the night is darker now,
   And the wind blows stronger;
   Fails my heart, I know not how;
   I can go no longer.'
   'Mark my footsteps, good my page;
   Tread thou in them boldly:
   Thou shalt find the winter's rage
   Freeze the blood less coldly.'

5. In his master's steps he trod,
   Where the snow lay dinted;
   Heat was in the very sod
   Which the Saint had printed.
   Therefore, Christian men, be sure,
   Wealth or rank possessing,
   Ye who now will bless the poor,
   shall yourselves find blessing.

O Come, O Come Emmanuel

Author Unknown
A traditional hymn from the 12th century
English translation by: John Mason Neale (1818-1866) in 1851
Adapted by: Thomas Holman Helmore (1811-1890) in 1854
Scripture Reference: Luke 1:32,33, 78,79,
Matthew 1:22,23, Isaiah 59:20

The words to this church hymn for the season of Advent are centuries old, dating from the medieval years, and the author and composer are unknown. A musical setting that would accommodate the stanzas and the refrain "Rejoice! Rejoice! Emmanuel shall come to thee O Israel" was formed out of some liturgical chants in the 1800's.

The original Latin version of the song did not include the now popular refrain. The hymn has now been translated into over 125 languages.

John Mason Neale translated the hymn from Latin into English in 1851. He revised his translation in 1853 and the hymn quickly became popular. The word Emmanuel translated means "God With Us".

John M. Neale was born in London, England, and became an accomplished linguist, and a prolific writer of essays, commentaries, books for children, and hymns. He is also known for his English translation of the traditional Christmas song "Good Christian Men, Rejoice", which was included in "Neale's Carols for Christmastide" in 1853.

Englishman, Thomas Helmore, adapted the current tune "Veni Emmanuel" around Neale's English translation and the hymn was published in Neale's and Helmore's work "Hymnal Noted" in 1854.

Helmore was born in Kidderminster, England, and became an English teacher and choir trainer. He was ordained a Congregational minister in 1840. He authored another carol collection titled "Carols for Christmas".

A later English translation of the third and fourth stanzas is credited to Henry Sloane Coffin (1877-1954) in 1916. Coffin was born in New York City and became a Presbyterian clergyman in1900. In 1910, he co-edited the song collection "Hymns of the Kingdom". He was pastor at the Madison Avenue Church in New York from 1905 to 1926, and President of Union Theology Seminary from 1926 to 1945.

Historical Setting For "O Come, O Come Emmanuel":

The first three Christian Crusades took place in the 12th century, about the time this hymn originated.

The famous Charge of the Light Brigade took place during the Crimean War, which began in 1854. Thomas Helmore adapted the music and text for this hymn that same year.

O Come, O Come Emmanuel

O Holy Night

Words by: Placide Cappeau de Roquemaure (1808-1877) in 1847
Composed by: Adolphe Charles Adam (1803-1856) in 1847
English translation by: John Sullivan Dwight (1813-1893) in 1855
Original French title: "Cantique de Noel"
Scripture Reference: Luke 2:7

"O Holy Night" is one of the best known French Christmas songs, along with "Angels We Have Heard On High". This French hymn was originally titled "Cantique de Noel". The text was by part-time poet, Placide Cappeau , in 1847. Cappeau was a commissionaire of wines by profession, and an occasional writer of poetry by avocation. Cappeau was able to present his verse to Adolphe Adam by means of having a mutual acquaintance with a family from Paris by the name of Laurey. This song is most often credited to Adolphe Adam in music books, and Cappeau is hardly ever mentioned as being the writer of this wonderful text.

Adolphe Charles Adam composed the music. Adolphe Adam was born in Paris and was primarily a French operatic composer. He wrote thirty-nine operas, fourteen ballets, and a total of 80 stage works, besides managing a theater and being a professor at the Paris Conservatory. Adam's composition was first performed at the 1847 Christmas Eve midnight mass in the church of Roquemaure, France. Church authorities frowned on the song, and one French bishop denounced it for its "lack of musical taste and total absence of the spirit of religion". Today, "O Holy Night" is noted for its beautiful words and melody, and is one of the most popular songs for singing as a solo at Christmas. The English words we use today, which changed the title to "O Holy Night", were written by a Boston Unitarian clergyman and musical authority named John Sullivan Dwight. Dwight became a Unitarian clergyman in 1832, but left the ministry after a short time, because his heart was in music and teaching. He became a teacher of music and Latin at the Brook Farm community. He founded "Dwight's Journal of Music" published from 1852 to 1881, and was instrumental in organizing the Boston Philharmonic Society in 1865, and the Professorship of music at Harvard in 1876. This hymn's English translation was published in 1855, while Dwight was editor of his "Journal of Music".

Historical Setting For "O Holy Night":

In 1847, when this hymn was being created, the U.S. was at war with Mexico, and the Mormons founded Salt Lake City.

This French hymn was first translated and published in English in the same year of 1855 that the French hymn "Angels We Have Heard On High" was first published.

Massachusetts and Delaware made Christmas a legal holiday in 1855.

O Holy Night

Hark! The Herald Angels Sing

Words by: Charles Wesley (1707-1788) in 1739
Composed by Felix Mendelssohn (1809-1847) in 1840
Arranged by: William Hayman Cummings (1831-1915) in 1855
Original title: "Hymn for Christmas Day"
Scripture Reference: Micah 5:2, Luke 2:14

This hymn is one of more than 6,500 hymns from the pen of Charles Wesley, brother of John Wesley (the founder of Methodism). Charles was born in Epworth, Lincolnshire, England, and was the 18th of 19 children born to Samuel and Susanna Wesley.

It is thought that Charles wrote these lyrics approximately one year after his 1738 conversion to Christianity. He was inspired to write this verse by the joyous chiming of bells in London as he walked to church. The text first appeared in "Hymns and Sacred Poems" in London in 1739. Wesley originally called his poem a "Hymn for Christmas Day", without really giving it a formal title. "Hark, how all the welkin (heavens) rings" was the original first stanza words by Wesley. The title and text were altered closer to its present form by the famous revivalist, George Whitefield (1714-1770), in his song collection of 1753 titled "A Collection of Hymns for Social Worship". A further text revision of the latter verses in the 1760's, by Martin Madan, completed the modern text we use today. Like many of Wesley's hymns, this text is a condensed course in biblical doctrine in poetic form.

The hymn text as we know it appeared in the New Version of the Natum Tate and Nicolas Brady Psalter in 1782 during Wesley s lifetime.

William H. Cummings, a noted English musician and scholar made the hymn setting of Mendelssohn s music, in 1855; 116 years after Wesley first penned his lyrics. He adapted a theme from the 2nd movement of Mendelssohn's "Festgesang" from 1840 (which was a cantata to commemorate the invention of the printing press). It was first published with the tune of "Mendelssohn" in Richard R. Chopes' "Congregational Hymn and Tune Book " of 1857.

Felix Mendelssohn was the German-Jewish composer of chamber music, pianoforte music, symphonies, and oratorios. He was born in Hamburg, Germany, but lived in Italy several years, and frequently traveled to England. His full name was Jakob Ludwig Felix Mendelssohn-Bartholdy. He made his first public piano performance in 1818. Mendelssohn founded the Leipzig Conservatory of Music, and is credited with developing modern conducting techniques.

Wm. Cummings was born in Devonshire, England. He was an accomplished vocalist, and professor of singing at the Royal Academy of Music from 1879-1896. He was the principal of the Guildhall School of Music and organist at Waltham Abbey in England, when he adapted Mendelssohn's melody with Wesley's hymn text.

Hark! The Herald Angels Sing

We Three Kings Of Orient Are

Written and Composed by: Rev. John Henry Hopkins Jr. (1820-1891) in 1857
Scripture Reference: Matthew 2:10,11

John Henry Hopkins, Jr., was born in Pittsburgh, and attended the "General Theological Seminary" in New York City, serving as the music instructor while he was there. Hopkins was also an author, journalist, illustrator, and designer of stained glass windows. His father was the Episcopalian Bishop of Vermont. From 1853 to 1868, John served as the editor of the "Church Journal". In 1857, this hymn was one of a number of selections he wrote for a Christmas pageant. The song was a favorite with Hopkins' nieces and nephews, and was first published in his "Carols, Hymns and Songs" collection of 1862. It gained popularity by being included in John Stainer's 1871 collection of "Christmas Carols New & Old". It's been widely used in carol services, because the dramatization of the biblical story from Matthew can be acted as well as sung.

The traditional names of the three kings were Melchior (ruler of Nubia and Arabia), Caspar of Tarsus, and Balthazar of Ethiopia. The gifts they presented to the Holy Child signified Jesus' kingship (gold), His oneness with God (frankincense), and His eventual death on the cross (myrrh). Hopkins served as rector at an Episcopalian church in Plattsburgh, New York from 1872 to 1876, and then as rector at the Williamsport, Pennsylvannia Episcopalian Church from 1876 to 1887.

"Gather Around The Christmas Tree" was another Christmas song authored by Hopkins, although it has remained in relative obscurity.

Historical Setting For "We Three Kings":

Booker T. Washington and Sigmund Freud had just been born the year before Hopkins wrote his song in 1857.

The hymn was published during the American Civil War in 1862. The Homestead Act of 1862 gave settlers 160 acres of Federal land if they would farm the land for five years.

When this hymn was gaining popularity in 1871, P.T. Barnum was organizing his circus billed as the "Greatest Show On Earth".

We Three Kings of Orient Are

Moderately

We Three Kings Of O - ri - ent Are; Bear - ing gifts we tra - verse a -
Born a King on Beth - le - hem plain, Gold I bring to crown him a -

far, Field and foun - tain, moor and moun - tain Fol - low - ing
gain, King for - ev - er, ceas - ing nev - er, O - ver us

Refrain

yon - der star. O_____ star of won - der, star of night,
all to reign.

Star with roy - al beau - ty bright, West - ward lead - ing,

still pro - ceed - ing, Guide us to thy per - fect light.

3. Frankincense to offer have I;
   Incense owns a Deity nigh;
   Prayer and praising, all men raising,
   Worship Him, God most high.
   (Refrain)

4. Myrhh us mine: it's bitter perfume
   Breathes a life of gathering gloom:
   Sorrowing, sighing, bleeding, dying;
   Sealed in the stone-cold tomb.
   (Refrain)

5. Glorious now, behold Him arise
   King and God, and Sacrifice!
   Heav'n sings alleluya,
   Alleluya the earth replies:
   (Refrain)

Jingle Bells

Written & Composed by: James S. Pierpont (1822-1893) in 1850
Original title: "The One Horse Open Sleigh"

James S. Pierpont was born in Boston, and became a popular composer. Pierpont performed this song for the first time in 1857 for a Thanksgiving program at the large Boston church where he taught Sunday school, and performed it again at Christmastime. It is reported that Pierpont actually wrote the song in 1850, and the original title was "The One Horse Open Sleigh". It was published under that title in Sept. of 1857, selling for 25 cents per copy and published for the first time under the name "Jingle Bells" in 1859. A friend of Pierpont's, Mrs. Otis Waterman, called the song a "merry little jingle" and helped give the tune the name by which we know it today. The original chorus music has been changed over time, but the words and the music for the verses has remained the same.

This was the first well-known American secular carol, however, the song did not acquire widespread popularity until the 20th century. The ironic aspect about this song becoming a favorite Christmas song is that there is no specific reference to Christmas in its lyrics.

Pierpont was the son of a prominent abolitionist, but he moved to Georgia, married a Southern girl and served in the Confederate Army. During the Civil War, Pierpont wrote rallying songs for the Confederacy.

Pierpont was the uncle of the American financier John Pierpont (J.P.) Morgan.

Historical Setting For "Jingle Bells":

A severe cholera epidemic plagued the Oregon Trail, and the American Express Company was organized the same year this song was written in 1850.

"Jingle Bells" was first published under the title "The One Horse Open Sleigh" in 1857. That same year, the Dred Scott decision held that a slave did not become free when taken into a free state.

The first territorial fair in the U.S. was held in Nebraska City, located in Nebraska Territory, in 1859, the same year that this song was first published as "Jingle Bells".

Jingle Bells

Up On The House Top

Written & Composed by
Benjamin Russell Hanby (1833-1867) circa 1860

This mid-19th century song by Benjamin Hanby was most likely inspired by Clement Clarke Moore's poem, "A Visit from St. Nicholas", written in 1822. Moore's poem, in turn, was influenced by the 1809 writing of Washington Irving when he pictured Santa Claus as a jolly, tubby little fellow who rode through the air in a sleigh drawn by reindeer.

As with most children since the 1820's, Hanby would have been well acquainted with Moore's poem as a young boy. No one before Moore had suggested that Santa's sleigh could land on a rooftop. The song has long been a favorite at school Christmas pageants as a choir song for children.

Hanby was born in Rushville, Ohio, and began writing popular songs while a student at Otterbein College in Westerville, Ohio. His 1856 song, "Darling Nelly Gray", did much to arouse sympathy for America's slaves. He graduated from Otterbein in 1858 and went on to pastor a United Brethren Church in Lewisburg, Ohio between 1861-63. Hanby worked for the John Church Music Co. in 1864, before moving on to the Root & Cady Music Co. in Chicago where he began working in 1865 and remained until his death. While there, he authored a collection of songs titled "Our Song Birds" which contained 60 of his tunes. No one has determined exactly when Hanby wrote this Christmas song. The period between the late 1850's, and mid 1860's, is the most likely

Hanby also authored a religious Christmas hymn titled "Who Is He In Yonder Stall" in 1866.

Historical Setting For "Up On The House Top":

Minnesota and Oregon had just become States.

Up on the Housetop

While Shepherds Watched Their Flocks

Words by: Nahum Tate (1652-1715) in 1696
Composed by: George Frederick Handel (1685-1759) in 1728
Adapted by: Richard Storrs Willis (1819-1900) in 1861
Scripture Reference: Luke 2:8-14

Nahum Tate was born in Dublin, Ireland, the son of an Irish clergyman, and later immigrated to England. He became a poet and playwright, and was appointed Poet Laureate of England by King William III in 1692. His hymn, written in 1696, was a metrical version of Luke 2:8-14 and was first published in 1700, in a supplement to a work by Tate and Nicholas Brady titled "New Version of the Psalms of David".

This hymn was originally sang to a tune by Thomas Este, known as "Winchester Old" in England. The tune by Este was first published in his "Whole Book of Psalms" in 1592. In 1708, Tate's hymn was the only Christmas song sanctioned by the Church of England for use in worship services.

Despite all of his musical and literary efforts, Tate failed to achieve financial success and died in a debtors' refuge. George F. Handel composed the tune used most often with this hymn in the United States. (As many as seven different tunes have been used for this hymn). Handel's familiar tune was taken from his opera "Siroe, Re di Persia" in 1728. Handel was the German composer, born in Halle, famous for his oratorio composition "The Messiah", in 1741. He wrote a total of 25 oratorios, 16 suites, 12 concertos, about 40 operas, and various other music. Although being born in Germany, Handel spent most of his life in England and became a naturalized English citizen in 1727.

Richard Storrs Willis, from Boston, put together the music of Handel, and text of Tate, in 1861, (165 years after Tate penned the words) resulting in the hymn as we know it today.

Historical Setting For "While The Shepherds Watched":

The lyrics were written in 1696, when Capt. William Kidd was hired by the British to fight pirates and take booty, but himself became a pirate.

The French were colonizing Louisianna in 1700 when this hymn was published.

Handel composed the music in 1728. This was a year after the death of Sir Isaac Newton. "Gulliver's Travels" was still a new literary work at this time.

Willis adapted the hymn in 1861, the same year that the American Civil War began, and the U.S. population was estimated at 32.4 million.

While Shepherds Watched Their Flocks By Night

Moderately

While_____ Shep - herds Watched Their
"Fear_____ not!" said he, for

Flocks By___ Night, All___ seat - ed on the___ ground,_____ The___
might - y___ dread Had___ seized their trou - bled___ mind,_____ "Glad___

an - gel of the Lord came__ down, And___ glo - ry shone a -
tid - ings of great joy I____ bring, To___ you and all man -

round,_____ And glo - ry shone a - round.
kind,_____ To you and all man - kind.

3. "To you, in David's town this day,
Is born of David's line,
The Saviour, who is Christ the Lord;
And this shall be the sign,
And this shall be the sign:

4. "The heavenly Babe you there shall find
to human view displayed,
All meanly wrapped in swathing bands,
And in a manger laid,
And in a manger laid."

5. Thus spake the seraph; and forthwith
Appeared a shining throng
Of angels praising God on high,
Who this addressed their song:

6. "All glory be to God on high,
And to the earth be peace;
Good will henceforth from heaven to men,
Begin and never cease!"

The Holly and the Ivy

Author Unknown
Traditional English carol from around 1700
Scripture Reference: Luke 2:7

The words to "The Holly and The Ivy" were published around 1830 in "A New Carol Book" printed in Birmingham, England, without credit going to any certain author.

The song is set to an old French melody, and was first published with music in 1861 by Joshua Sylvester, in his carol collection titled "Christmas Carols". Sylvester admitted that he had obtained it from "an old broadside", printed a century and a half since". The term "broadside" refers to a sheet of paper that carols were printed on for all the people to sing, as was the custom in England with Christmas songs. Each broadside usually contained three or more carols, were often illustrated, and sold for a penny.

The association of holly and ivy, as in this carol, dates back centuries, pre-dating Christianity, back to Roman times and the days of the Druids in Gaul. In early times, holly was symbolic for the male sex, and ivy was symbolic of the female sex. As Christian symbols, the Holly represents Christ, and the Ivy can represent Mary. Overall, this song is full of symbolism, and it has a curious blend of nature worship and Christianity.

In early times, Christians placed holly and ivy in their windows to indicate that Christ had entered the home. Even the English colonists on the Mayflower, in 1620, carried a supply of holly and ivy for table decorations and wreaths to be woven for the children. The fact that holly has been used so long and often at Christmas may have given us the color scheme of red and green we associate with the Christmas season.

Historical Setting For "The Holly and the Ivy":

When this carol made its first appearance around 1700, the estimated population of the American colonies was 262,000. The largest cities were Boston and Philadelphia with 12,000 people in each city.

The modern words to this carol were first published in 1830, the same year that Sarah Hale published "Mary Had A Little Lamb", and the estimated population of the U.S. was 12.8 million.

Kansas became a State in 1861, the year this carol was first published with music.

The American Civil War began in 1861.

The Holly and the Ivy

Silent Night

Words by: Father Joseph Mohr (1792-1848) in 1816
Composed by: Franz Xaver Gruber (1787-1863) in 1818
English Translation by: John Freeman Young (1820-1885) in 1863
Original German title: "Stille Nacht"
Scripture Reference: Luke 2:7-16

Father Joseph Mohr was inspired to write "Silent Night, Holy Night" after he was called out into the snow to bless a newly born baby in the home of one of his poorest parish-ioners. He was so filled with the spirit of the season and with the simple beauty of the mother and infant that when he returned to his study he wrote the poem we sing today. Joseph Mohr was born in Salzburg, Austria, the son of a musketeer (Joseph Mohr) and seamstress (Anna Schoiberin). He became a Roman Catholic priest in 1815 and served several parishes around Salzburg. In 1816, When Mohr wrote the German words to "Stille Nacht", he was serving as a priest in a pilgrimage church in Mariapfarr, Austria. It had been thought that Mohr wrote the song in 1818, but in 1995 an original manuscript was discovered, dated 1816, and is the only known existing manuscript sighed by Mohr in his own handwriting. On Christmas Eve, 1818, in the village of Oberndorf, in the Austrian Alps, Mohr asked Franz Gruber, the village schoolmaster and organist, to set his poem to suitable music for two solo voices, chorus, and guitar accompaniment. The guitar accompaniment was needed because the church organ had broken down. Within a few hours Gruber composed the simple melody that generations have loved ever since, and the song was sung that same evening in the St. Nicholas Church where Mohr served as assistant priest from August 1817 to October 1819. Franz Gruber, the third son of a linen weaver, was born in Unterweizburg, near Hochburg, Austria. He was a schoolteacher at Arnsdorf from 1807-1829, and starting in 1816, he supplemented his income by being the organist at St. Nicholas Church. The last thirty years of his life he served as choirmaster in Hallein. Gruber wrote over 90 musical compositions, but is best remembered as the composer for "Stille Nacht".

The song might never have traveled beyond the village where it was written, except that the organ repairman, Karl Mauracher, obtained a copy of the hymn and repeated it to others throughout the region, but without mention of the composer or poet. The hymn spread throughout the region of Tyrol, and became known as a Tyrolean Folk Song. Various performing groups such as the Strasser Children's Quartet began using the hymn in concert throughout Austria and Germany. The song was first published in a song collection "Vier Achte Tyroler-Lieder" in Dresden between 1828 and 1833. The song was first published in a German hymnal in 1838, first heard in the United States in 1839, when a family of Tyrolean (Austrian) Singers, the Rainers, used it during their concert tour, and first published in the United States in 1841. But, it wasn't until 1854 that the world learned the names of Gruber and Mohr. That year the King of Prussia,

Frederick Wilheim IV, first heard the song and instucted his royal court musicians in Berlin to find out the names of the author and composer. They inquired with monks at the St. Peter's monastery in Salzburg about the song's origin. It was the son of Franz Gruber who convinced them that the credit should go to Mohr and his father. John F. Young, an American Episcopal clergyman, from Pittston, Maryland, translated the song into English, in 1863. There have been at least eight different English translations of the hymn (including the first by Jane Montgomery Campbell in London in 1863), but Young's is the most widely used in the United States. His translation first appeared in Clark Hollister's "Service and Tune Book" of 1863. This same English version of "Silent Night" first appeared in an American "hymnal" in 1871, but it was not until "Great Hymns of the Church" was published in 1887 that Young's English translation of the song was officially attributed to him. Young served as Bishop of the State of Florida, beginning in 1867, and is also known as the editor of two hymnals, one published in 1861 and another in 1887 (published posthumously by John Henry Hopkins, Jr., the author of "We Three Kings".)

Historical Setting For "𝔖ilent 𝔑ight":

Illinois became a State in 1818, the year this song was written and composed.

Paul Revere died in 1818.

The third U.S. flag set the number of stripes at 13 in 1818.

Between 1828 and 1833 the Democratic Party took its name, U.S. railroad passenger service began, the process of making chocolate candy was developed, and the Braille alphabet for the blind was invented.

Queen Victoria of England had just begun her 63 year reign a year before Silent Night was published in 1838.

Daguerre invented the first "camera" in 1839.

The hymn was first published in the U.S. in 1841. The same year that the first emigrant wagon train for California left Independence, Missouri. The U.S. population was 17 million.

In 1863, this hymn was translated into English. The same year that West Virginia became a State, the Battle of Gettysburg was fought, slavery was outlawed in the U.S., the International Red Cross was founded, and Henry Ford was born.

Silent Night

Angels From The Realms of Glory

Words by James Montgomery (1771-1854) in 1816
Composed by: Henry Thomas Smart (1813-1879) in 1867
Scripture Reference: Luke 2:8,9   Matthew 2:2
Original title: "Good Tidings of Great Joy to All People"

James Montgomery was born at Irvine, Ayrshire, in Scotland, the son of Moravian missionaries to the West Indies, both of whom died while he was still a boy. Relatively few hymn writers have been laymen, but such was the case with Montgomery. He became the newspaper publisher and editor of the "Sheffield Iris" in 1774, a position he held for 32 years. Montgomery was a determined advocate of social reform. He was imprisoned twice for his outspoken articles on national issues, once for reprinting a song in commemoration of the fall of the Bastille, and then for printing an account of a riot in Shiffield. Montgomery was an abolitionist, supporter of the British Bible Society, and was closely associated with the efforts of evangelical Anglicans to win acceptance for hymn-singing in their churches.

"Angels From The Realms of Glory" is one of over 350 hymns written by this Scottish editor and hymn writer. It made it's first appearance as a poem in Montgomery's newspaper, "The Iris", on December 24, 1816. It became universally popular after its publication in the "Christian Psalmist" in 1825. For awhile, the hymn was known as "Good Tidings of Great Joy to All People", and until the 1867 tune was matched to Montgomery's song, the tune for "Angels We Have Heard On High" was used with it.

Henry T. Smart was an English sacred music organist, from London, England. He served as organist in four prominent London churches beginning in 1831. Smart's eyesight began to fail in 1864, and he was totally blind when he composed the music for this hymn in 1867, 51 years after Montgomery wrote the words. Smart titled his music "Regent Square", and dedicated it to London's Regent Square Presbyterian Church. Despite the disability of blindness the last 15 years of his life, Smart continued as organist at St. Pancras Church in London until his death in 1879.

Historical Setting For "Angels From The Realms of Glory":

King Shaka created the Zulu society and state in Africa in 1816, the same year this hymn made its first appearance in print as a poem.

The Erie Canal opened in 1825, when the hymn was first published with music.

Marie Curie was born in 1867, the year Henry Smart composed the modern music for this hymn.

Angels From The Realms Of Glory

Moderately

An - gels From The Realms Of Glo - ry, Wing your flight o'er
Shep - herds, in the field a - bid - ing, Watch - ing o'er your

all the earth, Ye who sang cre - a - tion's sto - ry,
flocks by night, God with man is now re - sid - ing;

Now pro - claim Mes - si - ah's birth. Come and wor - ship!
Yon - der shines the____ in - fant Light.

Refrain

Come and wor - ship! Wor - ship Christ the new - born King!

3. Sages, leave your contemplations,
brighter visions beam afar;
Seek the great Desire of Nations;
Ye have seen His natal star.
(Refrain)

4. See within a manger laid
Jesus, Lord of heaven and earth!
Mary, Joseph, lend your aid,
With us sing our Savior's birth.
(Refrain)

O Little Town of Bethlehem

Words by: Phillips Brooks (1835-1893) in 1868
Composed by: Lewis Henry Redner (1830-1908) in 1868
Scripture Reference: Luke 2:4, Micah 5:2

Phillips Brooks was born in Boston, the son of a merchant. He was a large man for his time, standing a tall 6'6". He became an Episcopal deacon in 1859 at the Church of the Advent in Philadelphia. He served as rector of the Holy Trinity parish in Philadelphia from 1862 to 1869. He gained national prominence for his preaching ability. In 1880, he became the first American to preach before a member of the English Royal Family (Queen Victoria). Brooks was also an abolitionist, and supported the Union cause during the Civil War. Three years after an inspirational trip to the Holy Land in 1865, he said the memory was "still singing in my soul" and he wrote the words to "O Little Town of Bethlehem" in 1868 for his Sunday school class of 36 kids to sing at a program. Brooks went on to serve as bishop of the Holy Trinity Church in Boston from 1869 to 1891. After that he served as the Bishop of Massachusetts until his death. Brooks was elected to the American Hall of Fame in 1910. Lewis H. Redner composed the music to Brooks's text in 1868, while serving as the organist and Sunday school superintendent for the Holy Trinity Church in Philadelphia. As with "Silent Night", the music for this hymn was composed within 24 hours of when it was first sang at a church program. The words and tune were hastily printed on leaflets and sung on Christmas morning by six Sunday school teachers and thirty-six children. Redner always insisted that the melody, which came to him during the night before the program, was "a gift from heaven". Lewis Redner was born in Philadelphia, Pennsylvania, and was a wealthy real estate broker and devoted churchman. He served as the Sunday school Superintendent at Trinity Church for 19 years.

The tune name for this hymn is "St.Louis", and it was first published with words in 1874, in a collection titled "Church Porch" by Rev William R. Huntington. Huntington is also credited with giving Redner's tune the name "St.Louis", which is a play on Redners first name. The hymns popularity was advanced by its inclusion in the Episcopal Church hymnal of 1892. Brooks and Redner teamed up on another little known Christmas song titled "Everywhere, Everywhere, Christmas Tonight". Brooks' first verse words to this song are:

Christmas in lands of the fir tree and pine,
Christmas in lands of the palm tree and vine,
Christmas where snow peaks stand solemn and white,
Christmas where cornfields lie sunny and bright.
Everywhere, everywhere, Christmas tonight!

O Little Town Of Bethlehem

Here We Come A Caroling

Author Unknown
Traditional English carol from the 17th century
Original title: "The Wassail Song"

This is an old English wassail song (a song to wish good health, which is what "wassail" means), believed to have originated from the north of England in the 17th century, although as with many of the traditional English carols, the author and composer have never been identified. One can almost imagine that these English carols were created by "groups of waits" coming up with new material to use for the Christmas season, and thus the songs were the product of early day "jam sessions" as we would call them today.

The oldest "broadside" in which the song is found is from circa 1850. The current text is found in "Songs of the Nativity" collection by William Henry Husk (1814-1887) in 1868. The current tune was arranged by John Stainer for his 1871 "Christmas Carols New & Old". Stainer arranged so many Christmas hymns for his 1871 collection of hymns, that he is often mistakenly credited as being the creator of the hymns.

The Christmas spirit usually made the English upper class a little more generous than usual, and the bands of beggars and orphans would dance through the streets of England, offering to sing good cheer if the householder would give them a drink from the wassail bowl, or some other treat. The wassail bowl was a combination of fermented hot ale or beer, spiced with cinnamon and ginger, and just alcoholic enough to keep the singers warm on their rounds. This old English custom of "wassailing" would be similar to American children dressing in costumes and going door to door for a treat at Halloween.

Historical Setting For "Here We Come A Caroling":

The King James Version of the Bible was published in the 17th century.

The Pilgrims established their Plymouth colony in America in the 17th century.

The potato chip was introduced in 1850, the year this carol made its first appearance on an English "broadside".

Abraham Lincoln proclaimed Thanksgiving a National Holiday in 1864, the year the modern text for this carol was published.

Lloyd's of London was founded in 1871. That year John Stainer arranged the current tune for this carol and published it in his "Christmas Carols New & Old".

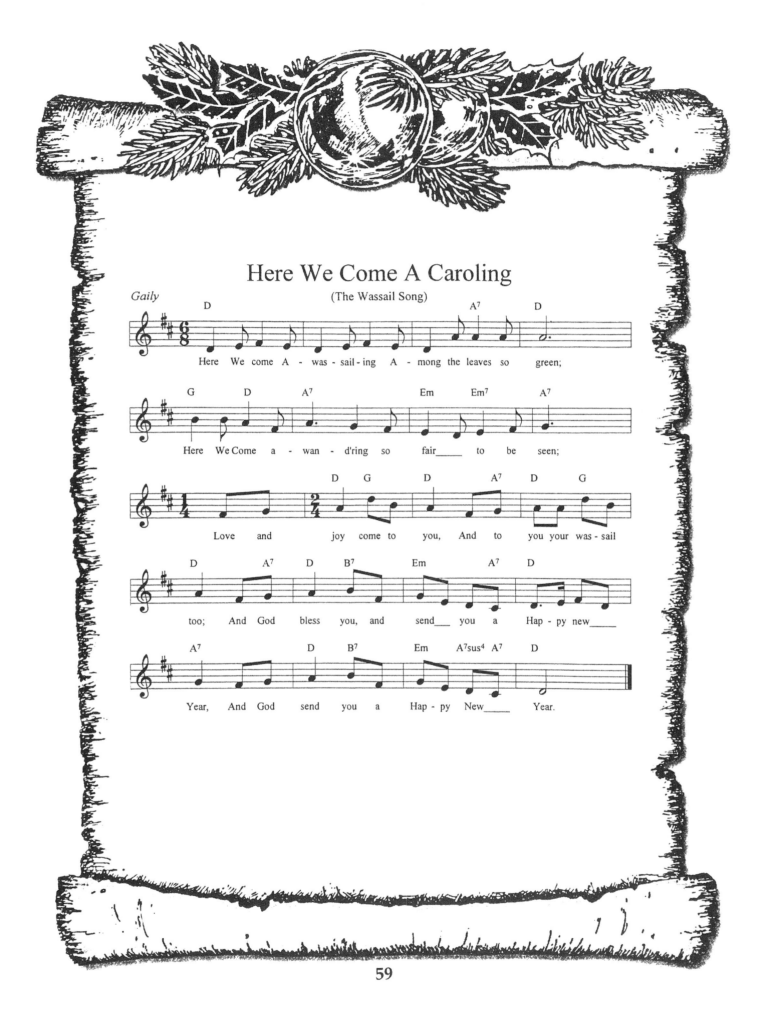

Here We Come A Caroling

(The Wassail Song)

God Rest Ye Merry Gentlemen

Author Unknown
Traditional English carol from the 16th century
Arranged by: Sir John Stainer (1840-1901) in 1871
Scripture Reference: Romans 8:38,39

This is possibly the best known carol of completely English origin, even though it's author and original composer remain totally anonymous. It was one of the carols that was sung by the municipal watchmen in old England who, like the town criers, were licensed to perform certain duties, such as singing seasonal songs to the proper people. The Old English word for "merry" meant pleasant or agreeable, not gay and lively as we think of it now, and Old English for "rest" meant "keep". So the Old English translation of this song title might be interpreted "God Keep You, Pleasant Gentlemen".

This carol is first found in written form in the collections known as the Roxburghe Ballads of 1770. The modern words were first published in "Facetiae and Miscellanies" by William Hone in 1827 as "an ancient version, sung in the streets of London". Charles Dickens used some of the words in his "A Christmas Carol", written in 1843. The melody is believed to be a folk melody from Cornwall in the west of England, and was first published in 1846 by Edward Francis Rimbault (1816-1876).

John Stainer, born in London, England, is credited with arranging the words to the music in 1871 (101 years after the words first appeared in print) giving us the carol as we are familiar with today.

Many of the traditional English carols were filled with "good tidings" to raise the spirits of the listener, such as this song with "tidings of comfort and joy...let nothing you dismay", and "love and joy come to you...and God bless you and send you a Happy New Year" as in "Here We Come A Caroling". What other time than Christmas can you find people at your front door singing you a musical blessing "for you and your kin"?

Historical Setting For "God Rest Ye Merry Gentlemen":

Ludwig Van Beethoven was born in 1770, the year this carol made its first appearance in print.

Ludwig Van Beethoven died in 1827, when the modern words to this carol were first printed.

Noah Webster would publish his American Dictionary the following year of 1828.

Charles Dickens used part of the carol in his "A Christmas Carol" in 1843.

The Smithsonian Institute was founded in 1846. The modern melody of this carol was printed that year.

Stainer arranged the carol in 1871 when English news correspondent, Henry Stanley, found Scottish missionary, David Livingstone, in Africa.

God Rest Ye Merry, Gentlemen

61

The First Noel

Author Unknown
Traditional English carol from the 13th century
Original English title: "The First Nowell"
Scripture Reference: Luke 2:8-2O

Unfortunately, the author and composer of this fine old Christmas carol have not been identified and most likely never will be discovered. "The First Noel" is considered a traditional English carol dating back as early as the 13th century, when the Miracle Plays (dramatizations of favorite Bible stories) were very popular. The song is viewed as a ballad carol for Epiphany, but is commonly sang at Christmas. The word "Noel" is the French word for Christmas and stems from the Latin "natalis", meaning "birthday". The original English song title was "The First Nowell", meaning "The First Christmas".

The first printed copy of the words appeared in "Some Ancient Christmas Carols" by Davies Gilbert in London in 1823. This carol collection by Gilbert is considered to be the first modern collection of any consequence to be published. William B. Sandys (1792-1874) first published the song with music in his 1833 London edition of "Christmas Carols, Ancient and Modern". The melody used by Sandys was basically the same as the one now in use. Sandys, an Englishman, is credited with pioneering popular interest in Christmas carols by his carol collection publications, which included "Christmastide, its History, Festivities, and Carols" in 1852. He was a lawyer, as well as a composer, and maintained a successful legal practice from 1814 to 1873.
John Stainer included his arrangement of the hymn in his 1871 "Christmas Carols New & Old", giving us the song as we know it today.

Historical Setting For "The First Noel":

The origins of this carol are traced back to the same time period that St. Francis of Assisi initiated the practice of using Nativity scenes (creches), in the 13th century.

The Monroe Doctrine went into effect in 1823, the same year that the words to this carol are first found in print.

The year 1833 saw the birth of Johannes Brahms, Alfred Nobel, and Benjamin Harrison. William B. Sandys published the words and music to "The First Noel" that year.

Slavery was outlawed in England in 1833.

The Dallas Theological Seminar was founded in 1871. John Stainer published the modern arrangement of this carol that year.

The First Noel

What Child Is This?

Words by: William Chatterton Dix (1837-1898) in 1865
Traditional tune: "Greensleeves"
Adapted by: Sir John Stainer (1840-1901) in 1871
Scripture Reference: Luke 2:17

William C. Dix was born in Bristol, England, the son of a doctor, and became the author of many poems. In 1865, Dix published "The Manger Throne" poem. Later, three stanzas were taken from that poem and fitted to the tune of "Greensleeves" by Sir John Stainer in 1871, thus creating the Christmas hymn "What Child Is This?" "Greensleeves" has a long history, dating back to the time of Henry VIII, and was first published in 1580. It was brought to America by the Pilgrims in 1620, and first published in 1642, in a carol collection titled "New Christmas Carols". The original words to "Greensleeves" are seldom used today.

Dix was an English marine insurance agent in Glasgow, Scotland. He wrote a large number of hymns, including another Christmas hymn, "As With Gladness Men of Old" in 1859.

Sir John Stainer was born in London, and became an eminent organist and composer in England. He was a chorister at the St. Paul's Cathedral in London from 1847 to 1856. He then served as the organist there from 1872 to 1888, until his eyesight began to fail. Stainer was knighted in 1888 and then became the professor of music at Oxford from 1889 to 1899. He served as the music editor for the 1871 collection "Christmas Carols, New and Old". This was the first major English language carol collection, and did much to promote carols of all types.

Historical Setting For "What Child Is This?":

English explorer, Sir Francis Drake, completed an around-the-world voyage in 34 months in 1580, the same year that "Greensleeves" was first published.

The Pilgrims brought "Greensleeves" to America in 1620.

When "Greensleeves" was published in America in 1642, the average transatlantic passage time for New England colonists averaged three months.

Dix wrote this verse the same year that the American Civil War ended, and President Lincoln was assassinated, in 1865.

Stainer arranged the carol in 1871, the same year that the Great Chicago fire devastated a 2,000 acre area and destroyed some 17,500 buildings.

What Child Is This?

Angels We Have Heard On High

Author Unknown
Traditional 18th century French carol
Original Title: "Les Anges dans nos Campagnes"
Scripture Reference: Luke 2:14-16

This is another favorite carol with an anonymous author. It is recorded that in 129 A.D., Telesphorus, the Bishop of Rome, ordained that "in the Holy Night of the Nativity of our Lord and Savior, all shall solemnly sing the "Angels Hymn". The "Angels Hymn" refers to the passages in Luke where the angels sing "Glory to God in the Highest, And on earth, peace to men of good will." The Latin version of the song begins "Gloria in excelsis Deo".

This hymn, as we know it today, was first published in a French carol collection titled "Nouveau Recueil de Cantiques" in 1855. The hymn was first translated into English in 1862 and published that year in "Crown of Jesus". The text is a translation of an old French carol "Les Anges dans nos Campagnes". Shepherds tending their flocks in the hills of southern France had a custom of calling to one another on Christmas Eve. The traditional tune the shepherds used is the refrain "Gloria in Excelsis Deo" we sing in "Angels We Have Heard On High". Richard Robert Chopes published the hymn complete with melody in his 1875-collection "Carols for Use In Church".

In England, this carol is called "Westminster Carol", from the fact that it is often sung in the Westminster Chapel during the Christmas season.

Historical Setting For "Angels We Have Heard On High":

The hymn was first published in 1855 when the Republican Party (GOP) was being formed.

The hymn was first translated in 1862. Billy Sunday was born that year, and the Morrill Act provided every State of the Union with public lands to be used for colleges.

The completed hymn was published in 1875. The first Kentucky Derby was held that year, and Albert Schweitzer was born.

Angels We Have Heard On High

2. Shepherds, why this jubilee?
   Sweetly singing o'er the plains,
   What the gladsome tidings be
   Which inspire your heavenly song?
   (Refrain)

3. Come to Bethlehem and see
   Him whose birth the angels sing;
   Come, adore on bended knee
   Christ the Lord, the newborn King.
   (Refrain)

4. See within a manger laid
   Jesus, Lord of heaven and earth!
   Mary, Joseph, lend your aid,
   With us sing our Savior's birth.
   (Refrain)

Deck The Halls

Author Unknown
Traditional Welsh carol
Original title: "Nos Galan"

Some believe that "Deck The Halls" was one of the jolly carols from the "Yule" celebrations in the British Isles, where Christians had adopted many of the Yule customs of the pagan Druids in one form or another. The "Yule" festival was celebrated about the same time of the year as Christmas, before Britain was Christianized. The Druids, (members of a pagan religious order in ancient Gaul, Briton and Ireland), used a burning Yule log to burn out the sins and evils of the past year. For Christians, the Yule log symbolized Christ as the Light of the World. The winter festival of Yule included the burning of the Yule log, decorating with holly and ivy, singing & dancing, feasting on plum puddings and mince pies, and drinking from the Wassail bowl.

The term "deck" dates back to the early 1500's, and it means to cover, array, or decorate. A favorite custom today is to array our homes with decorations at Christmas. The origin of the melody for "Deck The Halls" is unknown. Wolfgang Mozart used the melody in the mid-eighteenth century for a violin and piano duet. The song was first published in "Musical and Poetical Relicks of the Welsh Bards" with Welsh lyrics in London, in 1784, under the title "Nos Galan", meaning "New Years Night", however we do not know who wrote the original Welsh or American words.

The modern words are thought to be American in origin, but that is unknown for sure. The words were probably written in the 19th century when Charles Dickens' "A Christmas Carol" was at the height of its first popularity. The first known printing of the modern lyrics was in New York in 1881, in "The Franklin Square Song Collection" by J.P. McCaskey, and this advanced the popularity of the carol.

Historical Setting For "Deck The Halls":

This carol was first published with Welsh words in 1784. This was the first year after the American Revolution officially ended.

The first school for the blind was founded in 1784 (Paris). Clara Barton founded the American Red Cross in 1881, the year the English words to this carol were first published.

U.S. President Garfield was assassinated in 1881. The railroad reached Texas in 1881 and ended the famous cattle drives to Kansas.

Deck The Halls

2. See the blazing Yule before us,
   Fa la la la la, la la la la.
   Strike the harp and join the chorus,
   Fa la la la la, la la la la.
   Follow me in merry measure,
   Fa la la la la, la la la la.
   While I tell of Yuletide treasure,
   Fa la la la la, la la la la.

3. Fast away the old year passes,
   Fa la la la la, la la la la.
   Hail the new, ye lads and lasses,
   Fa la la la la, la la la la.
   Sing we joyous all together,
   Fa la la la la, la la la la.
   Heedless of the wind and weather,
   Fa la la la la, la la la la.

Away In A Manger

Adapted by: James Ramsey Murray
(1841-1905) in 1887
Original title: "Luther's Cradle Hymn"
Scripture Reference: Luke 2:7

This hymn is widely credited to Martin Luther, but he did not write this famous Christmas lullaby. The poem was first published, anonymously, in an 1885 children's Sunday school book in Philadelphia, titled "Little Children's Book".

James R. Murray published the verse in 1887 in a collection called "Dainty Songs for Lads and Lasses for Use in the Kindergarten, School and Home", and titled it "Luther's Cradle Hymn" for reasons unknown. The hymn has also been referred to as "The Children's Carol". At the time Murray was publishing this song he was serving as a music editor with the John Church Company in Cincinnati, where he worked from 1881 to 1905. Prior to that he had worked for the Root & Cady Music Co. until the Great Chicago Fire of 1871. The origin of the tune is uncertain, although it seems most probable that Murray was the composer. When the hymn was published again in 1888, there was a notation attached stating "Music by J.R.M.". James Murray was trained in music early in life, and became a music editor and hymn writer, composing a great number of Sunday school songs, gospel songs, and religious anthems. He was born in Ballard-Vale, Massachusetts, and was a veteran of the Union Army during the Civil War, however, he is best remembered for the hymn tune "Mueller" for "Away In A Manger".

John Thomas McFarland (1851-1913), a Methodist minister and educator, added the third stanza between 1904 and 1908 when an extra stanza was desired for use in a church children's program. McFarland served as President of Iowa Wesleyan University between 1884 and 1891. Beginning in 1904, he edited Methodist Sunday-school literature which he reformed and liberalized. It's during this time he added the third verse to this song. The words he used for the third stanza were first published in Charles Gabriels (1856-1932) collection "Vineyard Songs" from 1892.

Historical Setting For "Away In A Manger":

The first petroleum driven car took to the road in 1885, the same year the words to this hymn were first printed.

Coca-Cola had just been invented in 1886 and the Statue of Liberty was dedicated in October of that year.

Away In A Manger

Sweetly

A - way In A Man - ger, no crib for a bed, The
lit - tle Lord Je - sus laid down his sweet head. The
stars in the sky____ looked down where he lay, The
lit - tle Lord Je - sus, a - sleep on the hay.

2. The cattle are lowing, the Baby awakes,
   But little Lord Jesus no crying He makes.
   I love Thee, Lord Jesus, look down from the sky,
   And stay by my cradle till morning is nigh.

3. Be near me, Lord Jesus, I ask Thee to stay
   Close by me forever, and love me, I pray.
   Bless all the dear children in Thy tender care,
   And fit us for heaven to live with Thee there.

Jolly Old St. Nicholas

Author & Composer Unknown

If it was the desire of the author and composer of this Christmas song to remain anonymous...then the result was extremely successful. This American song was written sometime in the late 19th or early 20th century. Little else is known about this children's Christmas tune, however, the song's verses charmingly capture the anticipation of a visit by St. Nick.

In Holland and France gifts are put in children's shoes, if they are set out where Santa Claus can find them. In England he fills the children's stockings hung by the fireplace. In Germany and Scandinavian countries he hides the gifts away for the children to find. The verses of this song, and "Up On The Housetop", give an indication of how Santa brings gifts to children in the United States on Christmas Eve.

Some authorities have tried to associate Benjamin Hanby with this song, due to similarities in style with "Up On The Housetop", but this is merely conjecture at best. However, it would appear, at the very least, that Hanby's song influenced the making of this children's classic.

Jolly Old St. Nicholas

Moderately

Jol - ly Old Saint Ni - cho - las, Lean your ear this way! Don't you tell a

sin - gle soul What I'm going to say; Christ - mas Eve is com - ing soon;

Now you dear old man, Whis - per what you'll bring to me; Tell me if you can.

2. When the clock is striking twelve.
   When I'm fast asleep,
   Down the chimney broad and black,
   With your pack you'll creep;
   All the stockings you will find
   Hanging in a row;
   Mine will be the shortest one,
   You'll be sure to know.

3. Johnny wants a pair of skates;
   Susy wants a dolly;
   Nellie wants a story book;
   She thinks dolls are folly;
   As for me, my little brain
   Isn't very bright;
   Choose for me, old Santa Claus,
   What you think is right.

73

Toyland

Words by: Glen MacDonough (1870-1924) in 1903
Composed by: Victor Herbert (1859-1924) in 1903

This was one of the selections from Herbert's operetta, "Babes in Toyland", which opened in Chicago in June of 1903. Bessie Wynn and a male chorus introduced it. This same operetta also contained the well known Instrumental "March of the Toys". "Toyland" finds all the toys joining in for a tribute to their fabulous country, Toyland, and speaks about the great pleasure that toys bring to children. Victor Herbert was an Irish-American composer of more than 40 operettas. He was born in Dublin, Ireland, studied music in Germany, and came to America in 1886. He was a cellist, and conductor of the Pittsburgh Symphony Orchestra from 1898 to 1904, before becoming a composer. Herbert was a founding member of the American Society of Composers, Authors and Publishers (ASCAP). Glen MacDonough was born in Brooklyn, New York, the first of many 20th century Christmas music makers born in Brooklyn. He was one of the nine founders of the ASCAP publishing organization in 1914, along with Victor Herbert. MacDonough also collaborated with John Philip Sousa. Comedians Stan Laurel and Oliver Hardy brought this tale to the big screen with the 1934 film "Babes in Toyland".

Historical Setting For "Toyland":

Henry Ford founded the Ford Motor Co. in 1903.

The Wright Brothers made their famous flight at Kitty Hawk in 1903.

Professional baseball held its first World Series in 1903.

Toyland

Slowly

Toy - land! Toy - land! Lit - tle girl and boy - land.
Child - hood's joy - land, mys - tic mer - ry Toy - land!

While you dwell with - in it____ you are ev - er hap - py then.
Once you pass it's

bor - ders you can ne'er____ re - turn a - gain.____

There's A Song In The Air

Words by Josiah Gilbert Holland
(1819-1881) in 1872
Composed by: Karl Pomeroy
Harrington (1861-1953) in 1904
Scripture Reference: Luke 2:13

Josiah Holland was born into a poor family in Belchertown, Massachusetts. He became a skilled writer, editor and lecturer. Holland received a medical degree in 1844, but after brief careers in medicine, and teaching, he devoted his life to being a newspaper and magazine editor. He began his writing career by publishing his own weekly newspaper called the Bay State Courier in 1840 's. While serving as the co-editor of the Springfield Republican he wrote under the pseudonym of Timothy Titcomb. His writings flourished in the 1850's and 1860's, and in 1869 he co-founded "Scribners Magazine". In 1872, Holland penned the words to this popular Christmas hymn. The poem made it's first appearance in "The Marble Prophecy and Other Poems" in 1872.

Karl Harrington was born in Somersworth, New Hampshire. He became a classics scholar, and accomplished musician, serving as organist and choir director in various Methodist churches. Harrington wrote the music for this hymn while staying at his summer home in New Hampshire in 1904, thirty-two years after Holland wrote his lyrics. Harrington's hymn tune "Christmas Song", for Holland's text, came out in the 1905 edition of the Methodist Hymnal.

Historical Setting For "There's A Song In The Air":

Calvin Coolidge was born in 1872, the year this poem was written and published.

President Grant was re-elected for another term in 1872.

The Panama Canal construction began in 1904, the same year the music was composed for this song.

A Syrian vendor named Hamwi served the first ever ice cream cones at the St. Louis Fair in 1904.

Albert Einstein published his "Theory of Relativity" in 1905, the same year this song was first published.

There's A Song In The Air

Allegretto moderato

1. There's A Song In The Air! There's a star in the sky! There's a
2. There's a tu - mult of joy O'er the won - der - ful birth, For the

moth - er's deep prayer And a ba - by's low cry! And the
Vir - gin's sweet boy Is the Lord of the earth. Ay! the

star rains it's fire while the beau - ti - ful sing, For the
star rains it's fire while the beau - ti - ful sing, For the

man - ger of Beth - le - hem cra - dles a King!
man - ger of Beth - le - hem cra - dles a King!

3. In the light of that star
   Lie the ages impearled,
   And that song from afar
   Has swept over the world.
   Ev'ry hearth is aflame,
   and the beautiful sing,
   In the homes of the nations
   that Jesus is King!

4. We rejoice in the light,
   And we echo the song
   That comes down thro' the night
   From the heavenly throng.
   Ay! we shout to the lovely
   evangel they bring
   And we greet in His cradle
   our Savior and King!

Go Tell It On The Mountain

Author of the Refrain Unknown
Traditional spiritual
Stanzas by: John Wesley Work II (1871-1925)
Tune: Attributed to Frederick
Jerome Work (1880-1942)
Scripture Reference: Isaiah 40:9, Luke 14:23

This is one of the spirituals that originated with the slaves in the southeast United States. After the Civil War a man named William Francis Allen first collected spiritual songs and published them in a book in 1868 called "Slave Songs of the United States". This spiritual probably dates from the early 1800's, and was first popularized in 1879 by the Fisk University Jubilee Singers. This chorus traveled throughout the United States and Europe at the end of the 19th century, raising scholarship-fund money for Fisk, a school founded to educate freed slaves.

The author of this song's popular refrain is unknown. Today's tune has sometimes been attributed to Frederick Jerome Work (1880-1942), brother of John Wesley Work II, who wrote some of the modern stanza lyrics, and arranged the music. Frederick served as the music director at the New Jersey Manual Training School in Bordentown from 1922 to 1942. The brothers quite often collaborated on their musicals works, and in 1901, they published their first song collection titled "New Jubilee Songs As Sung By The Fisk Jubilee Singers".

John Work II, born in Nashville, Tenn., was a collector and interpreter of Negro spirituals, a longtime teacher at Fisk University, and served as the director of the Fisk Singers. In 1923 he became president of Roger Williams College in Nashville. "Go Tell It On The Mountain" was first published in "Folk Songs of the American Negro" in 1907 by the Work brothers.

Historical Setting For "Go Tell It On The Mountain":

The song was popularized in 1879, about the time that Thomas Edison was inventing the light bulb.

Oklahoma became a State in 1907, when this song was published.

The United Press news service was established in 1907.

Go Tell It On The Mountain

I Heard The Bells On Christmas Day

Words by: Henry Wadsworth Longfellow (1807-1882) in 1863
Composed by: John Baptiste Calkin (1827-1905) in 1872
Original title: "Christmas Bells"
Scripture Reference: Micah 5:5, Luke 2:14, Ephesians 2:14

The American poet, Henry Longfellow, was born in Portland, Maine. He was considered the most influential American poet of his day. He began publishing his poems in 1839. One of his best known works is "The Courtship of Miles Standish". After his son Charles was seriously wounded in the Civil War, and his second wife, Fanny, died in a fire, he turned to writing more spiritual topics. He penned "I Heard the Bells on Christmas Day" on Christmas Day, in 1863, and presented it to the Sunday school of the Unitarian Church of the Disciples in Boston. Reportedly, he was inspired to write the poem by the bells chiming out on Christmas. It was originally titled "Christmas Bells", and was first published by that title in a collection of poems entitled "Flower de Luce", in 1867. The original poem contained two verses that referred to the Civil War. The verses were written a mere six months after the Battle of Gettysburg. Longfellow had intended that the words to this song would remain only as a poem, and he would no doubt be surprised that it became a song.

As with several other famous people, such as George F. Handel, Felix Mendelssohn, Mel Torme, Eddy Arnold, Meredith Willson, and Adolphe Adam---Henry Longfellow's contribution to Christmas music is seldom mentioned in his biographies.

John Baptiste Calkin was born in London, and became a church organist and educator. He served as organist in various Chapels from 1853 to 1884. In 1872 he composed the hymn tune "Waltham", which was originally written for different words.

Today, another tune commonly sung to the words of Longfellow's poem was adapted by Johnny Marks in the 1950's.

Historical Setting For "I Heard The Bells On Christmas Day":

West Virginia became a State in 1863, the year Longfellow wrote this verse.

The Battle of Gettysburg was fought between July 1-3 in 1863

Nebraska became a State in 1867, the year this poem was first published.

Yellowstone National Park was established as the first National Park in the U.S., and Tree-Planting Day (later to become Arbor Day) had its origin in Nebraska, in 1872, the year that music was composed for this song.

Sweet Little Jesus Boy

Written & Composed by:
Robert MacGimsey (1898-1979) in 1932
Scripture Reference: Luke 2:7, Isaiah 53:3

The words to this lullaby are based on Scripture from Isaiah 53:3. Jesus, in his adulthood, would be despised and rejected by the world, a man of sorrows, acquainted with grief, and the world did not recognize His worth, just as Isaiah foretold 700 years before the birth of Jesus. Robert MacGimsey wrote this song on Christmas Eve, 1932, after taking a dispiriting walk past the crowded taverns and night-clubs of New York City.

MacGimsey was born in Pineville, Louisianna, and practiced law before becoming a professional whistler. He had the unique ability to whistle in harmony two or three tones simultaneously. He received his formal music education at the Juilliard School of Music.

MacGimsey's songs were composed in the dialect of the Louisiana Negro. His other best known original composition is "Shadrach".

Historical Setting For "Sweet Little Jesus Boy":

U.S. unemployment stood at 12 million men out of work in 1932.

The Empire State Building was only a year old in 1932.

The atom was split for the first time in 1932.

U.S. Route 66 from Chicago to Los Angeles opened in 1932.

Santa Claus Is Coming To Town

Words by: Haven Gillespie (1888-1975) in 1932
Composed by: John Frederick Coots (1897-1985) in 1932

Haven Gillespie and John Coots wrote this children's song in 1932, but no music publisher's were interested, because "kiddie" songs at the time were "uncommercial". Eddie Cantor's wife, Ida, persuaded him to try it out on his radio show, around Thanksgiving in 1934, and it was an instant hit. Only "White Christmas" and "Rudolph" have outsold this popular Christmas song, which actually was the first in a string of commercially successful Christmas songs over the next twenty year period.

Haven Gillespie was born in Covington, Kentucky, and left high school to become a journeyman printer. He worked for the New York Times and other newspapers. Gillespie went on to write songs for film, theatre, and radio.

J. Fred Coots was born in Brooklyn, New York, and got his start as a Vaudeville performer, pianist, and songwriter. He wrote music for a number of musical comedies. Another of his famous compositions was "Love Letters In The Sand".

Historical Setting For "Santa Claus Is Coming To Town":

Charles Lindbergh Jr. was kidnaped in 1932, the year this song was written and composed.

The United States, and the world, was in the midst of a Great Depression in 1932.

Prohibition came to an end the following year of 1933.

F.D.R.'s "New Deal" was getting off the ground in 1934 when this song debuted.

Winter Wonderland

Words by: Richard B. Smith (1901-1935) in 1934
Composed by: Felix Bernard (1897-1944) in 1934

This song from 1934 captures the enchantment of the winter season, making it a popular Christmastime tune. The endearing lyrics, by Richard Smith, and melody by Felix Bernard, provide a nice "pick-me-up" to the listener, and must have been like a "breath of fresh air" to the people living through the "dirty thirties", when the song first became popular. The Andrew Sisters had a big hit with the song in 1950, but the author and composer never lived long enough to hear it.

Richard Smith was born in Honesdale, Pennsylvannia. He served as an Editor-in-chief of a newspaper in Pennsylvania before taking up a career in music.

Felix Bernard was born in Brooklyn, New York. He got his start playing piano for music publishing houses and popular orchestras. He was a performer, pianist, tap dancer and writer of musical comedies in Vaudeville. Later he became a composer and conductor, and wrote material for Al Jolson & Eddie Cantor on radio shows.

Guy Lombardo was the first to record the song and it was number two on the Hit Parade of 1934.

Historical Setting For "Winter Wonderland":

This song was written and composed in 1934. On May 11th, 1934, a "Black Blizzard" of dust howled across the plains of the United States, scattering 300 million tons of soil as far as 300 miles out into the Atlantic ocean.

The U.S. Gold Reserve Act of 1934 authorized the president to revalue the dollar.

Flash Gordon and Li'l Abner comic strips debuted in 1934.

I Wonder As I Wander

Written & Composed by: John Jacob Niles (1892-1980) in 1933
Scripture Reference: Matthew 1:21

John Jacob Niles was a singer and collector of folk songs. He was born Jack Niles, in Louisville, Kentucky, studied music at the Cincinnati Conservatory, and went on to publish numerous books on folk music and ballads.

Niles devoted his life to not only collecting folk music, but also making musical arrangements for the songs of the Southern Appalachians.

He constructed his own instruments (dulcimers and lutes) for accompanying his singing. He based this song on a line or two of music that he heard sung by a young girl, Annie Morgan, in a small North Carolina town of Murphy. She was a member of a band of traveling evangelist and Niles listened to her sing the song without accompaniment. He reportedly asked her to sing the few notes over and over, paying her a few pennies each time, until he had jotted it all down in his notebook. The melody's minor key, minor intervals and unfinished rhythms, as well as the poem's pensive wording, make this one of the most melancholy and haunting of carols. Niles wrote the song in 1933 and the song was first published in Niles' 1935 publication "Ten Christmas Carols".

Historical Setting For "I Wonder As I Wander":

Franklin D. Roosevelt was elected President for his first term in 1933, the year Niles wrote this song.

The "gold standard" for backing U.S. money was stopped in 1933.

The Social Security Act was passed in 1935, the year this song was first published.

Will Rogers was killed in a plane crash in 1935.

𝔚𝔥𝔦𝔱𝔢 ℭ𝔥𝔯𝔦𝔰𝔱𝔪𝔞𝔰

Written & Composed by: Irving Berlin (1888-1989) in 1940

This Christmas classic was composed in 1940, and made its debut in the film "Holiday Inn" in 1942. It won the "Oscar" for best movie song in 1942 by the Academy of Motion Picture Arts and Sciences. This original version sung by Bing Crosby became the biggest selling commercial hit of all-time (a distinction it held until 1997), selling more then 31 million copies. It only took Crosby 18 minutes to record "White Christmas" as we know it today. There are now over 500 recorded versions of this song in dozens of languages. Berlin considered "White Christmas" the best song he ever wrote. The song was a particular favorite of the American troops stationed in the Pacific during World War II. Berlin said that "it became a peace song in wartime". Between 1942 and 1978 "White Christmas" had sold over 113 million records and 5.5 million copies of sheet music. In 1998 ASCAP announced it as the "most-performed" holiday song of the 20th century.

Irving Berlin was born in Tyumen, Russia, with the name, Israel Baline. His family came to America when he was four years old. His first hit song came in 1907, and he went on to become one of America's most prolific composers of musical scores for films and Broadway. His first major hit was "Alexanders Ragtime Band" in 1911. He wrote songs for the Ziegfeld Follies between 1919 and 1927. Berlin is also considered a pioneer of both ragtime and jazz music. Berlin never had any formal music training and he never learned to read or write music, but that did not keep him from becoming a highly successful producer of songs. He wrote "God Bless America" in 1918 and donated over six million dollars in royalties from the song to the Boys and Girls Scouts of America. In 1919, he founded the Irving Berlin Music Inc. Publishing Co.

Berlin (nicknamed Izzy) wrote and composed a second Christmastime song "Happy Holidays", which also debuted in the movie "Holiday Inn".

Historical Setting For "𝔚𝔥𝔦𝔱𝔢 ℭ𝔥𝔯𝔦𝔰𝔱𝔪𝔞𝔰":

The U.S. okayed the sale of surplus war material to Britain in 1940, the same year that Irving Berlin wrote this song.

The United States entered WWII in 1941.

When "White Christmas" made its debut in the wartime year of 1942, the first atomic reactor was being built in the U.S., and German U-boats sank 600 ships off the Atlantic coast of the United States and Canada.

I'll Be Home For Christmas

Words by: James Kimball "Kim" Gannon (19OO-1974) in 1943
Composed by: Walter Kent (1911-1994) in 1943

In 1943 the United States was at the midpoint of its participation in World War II, and many thousands of American men and women in the service would be spending Christmas far from home. The song was recorded by Bing Crosby and became an instant hit as it touched the hearts of those wanting to be home for Christmas, and the family members waiting back home for their loved ones to return. Kim Gannon was from Brooklyn, studied law, and was admitted to the New York Bar in 1934. He collaborated with John F. Coots, as well as Walter Kent, in writing songs for films and broadway.

Walter Kent was from Manhattan, New York, and recieved his formal music education from the Juilliard School of Music. He took advanced violin studies and for many years treated music as an avocation while studying and practicing architecture. At one time, Kent had his own orchestra that played on radio and in theaters. Kent was best known for his 1941 classic song "The White Cliffs of Dover". In 1943, he went to Hollywood to write songs for films.

Historical Setting For "I'll Be Home For Christmas":

United States troops invaded Italy in 1943.

Wage and salary earners became subject to a paycheck withholding tax in 1943.

American Broadcasting Co. (ABC) was founded in 1943.

Have Yourself A Merry Little Christmas

Words by: Ralph Blane (1914-1995) in 1944
Composed by: Hugh Martin (1914-   ) in 1944

This Christmas holiday tune was written as part of the musical score for the 1944 film "Meet Me In St.Louis", featuring Judy Garland. She made this song by Hugh Martin and Ralph Blane an instant success. In fact, it was Garland who influenced Blane and Martin to change some of the original words of the song from bittersweet to hopeful, and give us the lyrics we sing today.

Martin and Blane teamed up to do a number of Hollywood musicals. They also formed a mixed vocal quartet called "The Martins". Martin was born in Birmingham, Alabama, and became a composer, songwriter, and singer. He was the accompanist for Judy Garland at her first Palace Theatre performance, and started writing songs for Hollywood in 1943. Martin served in the Armed Forces during WWII.

Blane was from Broken Arrow, Oklahoma and his full real name was Ralph Uriah Hunsecker. He began his music career in radio and night clubs. Blane became a composer of Broadway musicals, TV shows and choral works. He became active in Hollywood after 1943.

Historical Setting For "Have Yourself A Merry Little Christmas":

The D-Day invasion of Normandy took place in 1944.

The G.I. Bill of Rights was signed into law in 1944.

The Federal Highway Act of 1944 established a new U.S. National System of Interstate Highways.

Let It Snow, Let It Snow, Let It Snow

Words by: Sammy Cahn (1913-1993) in 1945
Composed by: Jule Styne (1905-1994) in 1945

This wintertime song by Sammy Cahn and Jule Styne was written in 1945, and popularized by Vaughn Monroe in 1946. Its wording talks about the bitter weather outside, while expressing the pleasure of staying cozy by a warm fire inside.

Most of our favorite Christmas songs since the 1940's have been created by song-writing duo's. It became a trend for composers and lyric writers to team up in an effort to supply the music needed for Broadway shows, Hollywood films, and popular music recordings. Both Cahn and Styne were very successful in American popular music over a period of three decades.

Sammy Cahn (Samuel Cohen) was born in New York City and got his start in Vaudeville. Early in his career he played violin in variety shows. He went to Hollywood in 1940 to write film scores, and in 1955 he founded the Sammy Cahn Music Publishing Co. Cahn won Academy Awards for the "Best Song of the Year" in 1954, 1957, 1959 and 1963.

Jule Styne was born in London and came to the U.S. in 1913. His real name was Julius Kerwin Stein. In the 1920's he became interested in popular music and became a pianist with a dance band, later organizing his own orchestra. He wrote songs for movies during the 1930's. In 1942 he went to Hollywood and became a successful composer, publisher, and producer of musicals and plays, mostly comedies. He won an Academy Award (along with Cahn) for "Three Coins in the Fountain", voted the "Best Song of the Year" in 1954.

Historical Setting For "Let It Snow, Let It Snow":

The United Nations was established in 1945.

The first use of atomic bombs took place in 1945.

WWII ended in 1945.

Here Comes Santa Claus

Words by: Gene Autry (1907-1998) in 1946
Composed by: Oakley Haldeman (1909-1986) in 1946

This is one of three Christmas songs that Gene Autry helped to popularize, and which helped make Autry a famous singer of more than cowboy and country songs.

The song was created in 1946 by Autry and Oakley Haldeman, then published and recorded by Autry in 1947. Oakley Haldeman was a composer and music publisher from Alhambra, California.

Orvon Gene Autry was born in Tioga, Texas, and among many other things he achieved in his career, he became a motion picture star in 1934, and was the "Singing Cowboy" in 91 films through the 1950's. He was encouraged to pursue a career in singing by Will Rogers, after a chance meeting in a telegraph office where Autry was working in 1928. Autry received the first "Gold Record" ever presented to a singer for his million selling recording of "That Silver Haired Daddy Of Mine". He served his country in the Army during WWII from 1942-1945.

In the early 1950's, Autry turned his attention to building a business empire, including the ownership of radio and television stations, recording and publishing firms, movie studios, and the California Angels baseball team. He is the only person with five stars on the Hollywood "Walk Of Fame" for achievements in various careers. Autry even had a town in Oklahoma (about twenty miles from where he grew up) named after him in 1941.

Autry was inspired to write "Here Comes Santa Claus" after participating in a Christmas parade and hearing all the children say "Here comes Santa Claus! Here comes Santa Claus!" as they saw a float approach with Santa Claus. After the parade, Autry went back to his office and created the song. The lyrics for this song are unique in that they mention God, the Lord, and Santa Claus within the same song.

Historical Setting For "Here Comes Santa Claus":

The Philippines were given independence in 1946.

In 1946, the world was busy picking up the pieces and recovering from WWII.

Timex watches were introduced in 1946.

The Christmas Song

Words by: Robert Wells (1922-   ) in 1946
Composed by: Mel Torme (1925-1999) in 1946

This song is known most frequently by it's first line "Chestnuts Roasting on an Open Fire", but occasionally is referred to by the title "Merry Christmas To You". It was written by singer and entertainer, Mel Torme, and Robert Wells in 1946, about the indoor and outdoor joys of the Yuletide season.

Melvin Howard Torme was born in Chicago, Illinois, and was known as the "Velvet Fog" for his distinctive vocal qualities. He began to sing in vaudeville at an early age and was making records by the time he was in high school. Torme organized his own swing ensemble called the Mel-Tones. During WWII, Torme interrupted his career to enter the service in 1944. Torme recorded his song in 1946, and Nat King Cole recorded an even more successful version a decade later. Torme composed more than 300 songs in his career.

Robert Wells was from Raymond, in Washington State, and is the creator of a number of pop songs, cabaret acts, TV shows, and movie scores. His full name is Robert Wells Levinson.

The song was written and recorded in the middle of a summer heat wave. Wells had tried to beat the heat by jotting down some winter time thoughts on a spiral pad at his piano. Torme was instantly intrigued by the four lines that Wells had written and within 40 minutes the song as we know it was created, with Torme composing the music and some of the lyrics.

Historical Setting For "The Christmas Song":

The television era had just began, with the sale of T.V. sets increasing dramatically in 1946.

The first purely electronic computer came into use in 1946.

The two-piece bikini was introduced in 1946.

Ring Christmas Bells

Words by: Minna Louise Hohman in 1947
Composed by: Mykola Dmytrovich Leontovych (1877-1921) in 1916

This song was published in 1947. M.L. Hohman, an American from Chicago, added new lyrics to an often used tune by Ukranian composer, teacher and conductor, Mykola Leontovych. The tune has been used for four other Christmas carols over the years, including the "Carol of the Bells". Hohman wrote and adapted words for a number of songs with traditional tunes in a collection titled "Christmas In Song" in 1947. Leontovych, born in the Podilia Region of the Ukraine, composed the music in 1916 for a choral work called "Shchedryk", which was based on the Slavic legend that at midnight on the night Jesus was born, every bell in the world rang out in his honor. For centuries now, church bells in every land have pealed forth the glad tidings of the birth of Jesus with joyous ringing at Christmas. Leontovych's music was originally united with the text to "Carol of the Bells", written by Peter J. Wilhousky (1902-1978) in 1936. Wilhousky was a composer, lyricist and conductor from New Jersey.

An interesting Christmas custom in Leontovych's homeland of Ukraine was the observance of a thirty-nine day fast which ended on Christmas Eve with a twelve course dinner---one course for each of the twelve apostles of Jesus.

Historical Setting For "Ring Christmas Bells":

The U.S. bought the Virgin Islands from Denmark in 1916.

The Soil Conservation Act was passed in 1936.

The Dead Sea Scrolls were discovered in 1947.

Blue Christmas

Words by: Jay W. Johnson (1903-1986) in 1948
Composed by: Billy Hayes (1906-   ) in 1948

Billy Hayes and Jay Johnson wrote this Christmastime tune in 1948. The song first gained popularity with the Country & Western music audience. Most Christmas songs are filled with warmth, hope and good cheer, but this song speaks about being alone at Christmas, without the people you love. Billy Hayes was born in New York City, and was a vocalist, guitarist, and nightclub performer. Ernest Tubb had a number one recording with it in 1949. Elvis Presley's 1964 single of this song is one of the most popular Christmas recordings of all-time. In 1968, Elvis proclaimed "Blue Christmas" his favorite Christmas song.

Jay Johnson was born in the small town of Ellis, in western Kansas, and was a Vaudeville and nightclub performer. He was in show business for over 55 years, and collaborated with Harry Simeone, as well as Billy Hayes and others. In 1998, ASCAP (American Society of Composers, Authors & Publishers) ranked "Blue Christmas" in their top 25 holiday songs.

Historical Setting For "Blue Christmas":

The Organization of American States was founded in 1948.

Mohandes Gandhi was assassinated in 1948.

The Honda motorcycle was introduced in 1948.

Rudolph the Red Nosed Reindeer

Written & Composed by: Johnny D. Marks (1909-1985) in 1949

From a sales and merchandising viewpoint, this is one of the most successful songs (of any kind) of all time. It's the second biggest-selling recording (having sold over 25 million copies) after Bing Crosby's version of "White Christmas". "Rudolph" was introduced to the world by Gene Autry at Madison Square Garden in New York City in 1949. When Autry initially balked at recording the song, because it wasn't one of his favorites, his wife, Ina, encouraged him to sing it, intuitively sensing promise in its future popularity.

Johnny Marks was born at Mt. Vernon, New York, and studied music in Paris. He produced army shows during World War II and then in 1949, he formed the St. Nicholas Music Publishing Co. Over the years, he had a hand in creating or arranging more Christmas songs than any other single person. "Rudolph" was actually created by Robert L. May, a brother-in-law of Johnny Marks, and an advertising copywriter for Montgomery Ward, who made him the hero of a story pamphlet to be given away in the stores at Christmastime. The pamphlet was a success for 10 years before Marks wrote the song. After Marks could not convince anyone to publish or record the song, he formed his St. Nicholas Music Publishing Co., got Gene Autry to sing it, and the rest of the story, as they say, is history.

The animated TV special of "Rudolph The Red Nosed Reindeer" is the longest running television special to air on an annual basis since its first broadcast in 1962.

Historical Setting For "Rudolph the Red Nosed Reindeer":

Babe Ruth had died in 1948, the previous year this song was written.

Peter Marshall, Chaplain to the U.S. Senate during WWII, died in 1949.

The world population was estimated at 2.5 billion people in 1949.

C-H-R-J-S-T-M-A-S

Jenny Lou Carson (1915-1978) in 1949
Composed by: Eddy Arnold (1918-   ) in 1949
Scripture Reference: Luke 2:7-16, Matthew 2:9-11

Country singers and songwriters, Eddy Arnold, and Jenny Lou Carson wrote this song in 1949. It makes an acronym of the true symbols of Christmas, and reminds us of the day's true meaning. Carson was one of the most active songwriters of "morale boosting" material during WWII, and Eddy Arnold recorded a number of Carson's songs. She was born, Lucille Overstake, in Decatur, Illinois, and did not change her name until the 1940's. Carson was elected to the Nashville Songwriters Hall of Fame in 1971. Jenny Carson, Katherine K. Davis, and Minna Hohman could be considered "pioneers" for women in the field of writing Christmas songs. Contributions by women in the making of Christmas music was virtually non-existent before the 40's. Eddy Arnold was born Richard Edward Arnold, on a farm near Henderson, Tennessee. As a young boy he admired singers like Bing Crosby, and especially Gene Autry. In 1940, Arnold became a popular singer on the "Grand Ole Opry", and eventually was nicknamed the "Tennessee Plowboy". He signed with RCA records in 1945, and got his first major TV break in 1949 when he appeared on the Milton Berle show. Arnold collaborated with Steve Edward Nelson and Ed Nelson, Jr. on another lesser known Christmas song "Will Santy Come To Shanty Town".

Historical Setting For "C-H-R-J-S-T-M-A-S":

NATO was established in 1949.

O'Hare Airport in Chicago received its name in 1949.

Silly Putty was introduced in 1949.

Silver Bells

Words by: Ray Bernard Evans (1915-   ) in 1950
Composed by: Jay Harold Livingston (1915-   ) in 1950

This 1950 Christmastime standard by Jay Livingston and Ray Evans debuted in the film "The Lemon Drop Kid". Bob Hope sang the song as part of a duet in the movie. "Silver Bells" was only one of many songs that this songwriting duo collaborated on for over a hundred Hollywood films. Ray Evans was born in Salamanca, New York. He received a Bachelor of Science degree in Economics. One of his early career jobs was performing as a musician on cruise ships. Jay Livingston was born in Mc Donald, Pennsylvannia. He majored in journalism at the University of Pennsylvannia. Jay also played on cruise ship bands with his college buddy, Evans, before going to Hollywood in 1945 to write songs for motion pictures. Both Livingston and Evans were under contract with Paramount from 1945-56 before freelancing for other Hollywood studios. Together they won Academy Awards for the "Best Song of the Year" in 1948, 1950 and 1956. They also wrote the theme song for the TV show "Bonanza". Regarding "Silver Bells", Ray Evans stated that "the main reason this song became so successful is that this is the only song...that's about Christmas in a big city with shop lights and shoppers and the rest...we got that only because that happened to be the locale of the picture." The title for the song was inspired by a small bell that Evans and Livingston noticed on a desk when they began working on the song. The intended original title "Tinkle Bells" was changed because Evans' wife found the proposed title to be too funny. "Silver Bells" became a favorite Christmas song of President John F. Kennedy.

Historical Setting For "Silver Bells":

The Korean War began in 1950. "Silver Bells" was created and debuted that same year.

The World population was estimated at 2.5 billion people in 1950.

The first credit cards were issued by the Diner's Club in 1950.

Sleigh Ride

Words by: Mitchell Parish (1900-1993) in 1950
Composed by: Leroy Anderson (1908-1975) in 1948

Leroy Anderson composed "Sleigh Ride" in the midst of a sweltering August heat wave in 1948. Mitchell Parish added the lyrics two years later. The song was first performed by Arthur Fiedler and The Boston Pops Orchestra. It was originally an instrumental piece, and is still frequently performed without the words.

Mitchell Parish was born in Shreveport, Louisianna, and became a prolific lyric writer for many years. He began writing poetry and short stories in school, and early on he had ambition to study medicine. He was working as a admitting clerk in a New York hospital when a doctor brought his verse to the attention of a music publisher. Later, he became a staff writer for a music publisher in 1919, and is credited with writing lyrics for more than a thousand songs. Parish collaborated with many composers, including Duke Ellington and Glenn Miller, however, he specialized in working alone and adding lyrics to pre-existing music. Leroy Anderson was born in Cambridge, Massachusetts. He received a Master of Arts degree from Harvard in 1930. Among other things, he served as a church choirmaster and organist from 1929 to 1935. During World War II, he served as a translator of Scandinavian languages, while serving in the Military Intelligence Service between 1943 and 1946. Anderson went on to become one of America's most gifted semi-classical composers.

Historical Setting For "Sleigh Ride":

Israel gained its independence from British rule in 1948, the year this tune was composed.

The Korean War began in 1950, the year the words were written for "Sleigh Ride".

Texaco Star Theatre was the number one rated TV show in 1950.

Frosty The Snowman

Words by: Walter E. "Jack" Rollins (1906-1973) in 1950
Composed by: Steve Edward Nelson (1907-1981) in 1950

Gene Autry recorded "Frosty" in 1950. This song by Steve Nelson and Jack Rollins, was written in 1950, and added a snowman to the list of characters without whom a modern Christmas can never be quite complete. As with "Rudolph", Frosty the Snowman was featured in his own animated television special. Part of the enchantment of this song is that it contains elements of a fairy tale.

Rollins was born in Scottdale, Pa., and Nelson in New York City. They also created the musical holiday character, Peter Cottontail in 1949. Nelson specialized in composing children and holiday songs. He wrote the official "Smokey the Bear" song for the U.S. Forestry Department. Nelson also co-authored a lesser known Christmas song titled "Will Santy Come to Shanty Town?" with his brother Ed Nelson Jr. and Eddy Arnold. Steve Nelson is a member of the Nashville Songwriters "Hall of Fame".

Historical Setting For "Frosty The Snowman":

Israel proclaimed Jerusalem as its capital city in 1950, the year this song was written and composed.

Smokey the Bear became a symbol for forest fire prevention in 1950.

The 22nd Amendment was added to the Constitution in 1951. It limits U.S. Presidential terms to two.

Willie Mays joined the New York Giants lineup, and Mickey Mantle debuted with the New York Yankees in 1951, the year this song gained popularity.

It's Beginning To Look Like Christmas

Written & Composed by: Meredith Willson (1902-1984) in 1951

Meredith Willson was born in Mason City, Iowa, and his real name was Robert Reiniger Willson. He is most famous as being the composer of "The Music Man", a smash Broadway hit in 1957. Before that, however, he had written this popular Christmas song in 1951. Willson wrote the song between the time he composed scores for motion pictures in the 1940's, and Broadway musicals in the 1950's and 1960's. He used the song as an important theme song in his Christmas musical on Broadway "Here's Love" in 1963. This musical was based on the movie "The Miracle on 34th Street". Bing Crosby recorded this song about holiday decorations the same year that Willson composed it. Willson studied music at the Institute of Musical Art (now the Juilliard School of Music). Between 1921 and 1923, Willson played first flute in the John Philip Sousa Band. He became a respected musical director for radio shows beginning in 1929. Willson also wrote the well-known songs "76 Trombones" and "Chicken Fat". In 1982, he was elected to the Songwriters Hall of Fame.

Historical Setting For "It's Beginning To Look Like Christmas":

General Douglas MacArthur was removed from command in Korea by President Truman in 1951.

Transcontinental television began with an address by President Truman in 1951.

Korean peace talks began in 1951, but the war continued for two more years.

There's No Place Like Home For The Holidays

Words by: Al Stillman (1906-1979) in 1954
Composed by: Robert Allen (1927-   ) in 1954

This song was published in 1954 and made popular by Perry Como. It's sentimental lyrics make it a natural favorite during the Christmas holiday, as people's thoughts turn toward home, and the love and friendship found in the company of family and friends. This is one of the best songs to listen to for recalling those memories of past family Christmas gatherings.

Al Stillman and Robert Allen combined to produce a string of popular music hits in the 1950's. Al Stillman was born in New York City, and was a staffmember of the Radio City Music Hall beginning in 1933. He was the author of many verses used in newspapers and magazines. Robert Allen was born in Troy, New York, and began his music career as a pianist in nightclubs. He created special material for Carnegie Hall performances, and also wrote the football march for Auburn University.

Historical Setting For "Home For The Holidays":

The U.S. Supreme Court ordered the states to begin desegregation in 1954.

The Fellowship of Christian Athletes organization was founded in 1954.

The first successful organ transplant took place in 1954.

"Under God" was added to the wording of the Pledge to the Flag in 1954.

The Little Drummer Boy

Written & Composed by: Katherine Kennicott Davis (1892-1980) in 1941
Original title: "Carol of the Drum"
New words by: Henry V. Onorati (1912-1993) in 1958
Composed by: Harry Simeone (1911-   ) in 1958

This song was originally written by Katherine K. Davis in 1941, and was titled "Carol of the Drum". Davis was born in St. Joseph, Missouri, became a music teacher, and was a respected composer of serious music including operettas and hymn tunes. Regarding this song, Davis said that the music came first and "the words seemed to come along with it". The carol was re-titled by Harry Simeone and Henry Onorati, "The Little Drummer Boy" in 1958.

Henry Onorati was born in Revere, Massachusetts, and was President of 20th Century Fox Records from 1958 to 1963. Harry Simeone was born in Newark, New Jersey, and was a one time choral conductor-assistant for Fred Waring, beginning in 1939. This song was recorded by the Harry Simeone Chorale on a 1958 Christmas album called "Sing We Now of Christmas". It tells of a shepherd boy who makes his way to the manger in Bethlehem to see the Christ child, and plays his drum for Jesus, since he has no finer gifts to offer.

Historical Setting For "The Little Drummer Boy":

Davis wrote the song the year the U.S. entered WWII in 1941.

The first U.S. domestic jet airline passenger service began in 1958, the year this song gained its new title.

NASA was created in 1958, and Explorer I became the first U.S. satellite to go into orbit.

Gunsmoke was the number one rated TV show in 1958.

Honorable Mention Christmas Songs

The following is a list of Christmas songs prior to 1960 that are worthy of mention
with a brief description about their origin.

(All I Want For Christmas Is) My Two Front Teeth
Written & Composed by Don Gardner in 1946

A novelty song, which was first heard on the Perry Como radio show, performed by a
singing group called "The Satisfiers". Spike Jones had a hit recording with the song in 1948.

What Are You Doing New Year's Eve
Written & Composed by Frank Loesser

Frank Loesser, a composer of multiple Broadway hits, wrote this Christmas song in 1947
and it was recorded that same year by Margaret Whiting.

I Saw Mommy Kissing Santa Claus
Written & Composed by Tommie Connor in 1952

This Christmas song would fit into a group of songs to be considered "novelty" pieces.
Twelve year old Jimmy Boyd recorded this song for Tommie Connor in 1952 and it went
on to sell nearly 2 million copies the first year.

Jingle Bell Rock
Written & Composed by Joe Beal and Jim Boothe in 1957

Joe Beal, a New England-born public relations man, collaborated with Jim Boothe, a
Texas writer in the advertising business, to create this Rock N' Roll novelty song, which
became a best-selling record for singer Bobby Helms exactly 100 years after James
Pierpont's classic Christmas song "Jingle Bells".

Rockin' Around The Christmas Tree
Written & Composed by Johnny Marks in 1958

Another of many Christmas songs composed by Johnny Marks. Brenda Lee had a big
hit with the song in 1958 and it was just one of a group of Rock N' Roll Christmas songs
to make the Billboard charts in the late 1950's

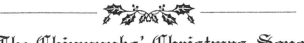

The Chipmunks' Christmas Song
Written & Composed by David Seville in 1958

A novelty song that was the brainchild of David Seville in September of 1958. He
thought of a melody on the way to work, went right to the studio and whistled the
melody into a tape machine so he wouldn't forget it. Seville provided the voices for
Alvin, Theodore and Simon by recording his own voice at half speed, then playing it
back at normal speed. The "Christmas Song" gave birth to the Chipmunk theme.

Christmas Music Trivia Questions

1. Who is known as the "Father of Caroling"?
2. When did street caroling originate?
3. Which song author was "Poet Laureate of England"?
4. Which song title represents the male & female sex?
5. Which song author wrote over 6,500 songs?
6. Which was the only Christmas hymn allowed for use by the Church of England in 1708?
7. Which song author barely stood 5' tall?
8. Which song author stood 6'6" tall?
9. What was the original Latin title for O Come All Ye Faithful?
10. When are the 12 days of Christmas?
11. What 19th century childrens story influenced future Christmas songs?
12. What song did Charles Dickens use in his 1843 "A Christmas Carol"?
13. What is the German language title for "Silent Night"?
14. Which famous American poet wrote "I Heard The Bells On Christmas Day"?
15. Which song was mistakingly credited to Martin Luther?
16. George Frederick Handel composed the music used with "While Shepherds Watched Their Flocks" and what other famous Christmas oratorio?
17. Who was the blind composer of "Angels From The Realms of Glory"?
18. What was a common practice during the 12 days of Christmas?
19. What were public singers & musicians called in 17th century England?
20. On what day in 1818 did Joseph Mohr ask Franz Gruber to compose the music for "Silent Night"?
21. In what country did the song "O Christmas Tree" originate?
22. What title did Isaac Watts earn?
23. Which was the 1st American Christmas song to achieve international fame?
24. What nationality was John Francis Wade?
25. "O Come, O Come Emmanuel" is a popular song for use during?
26. "The First Noel" is a popular song for use during?
27. The word "Noel" means?
28. Which two famous Christmas songs originated in France?
29. A visit to Bethlehem inspired Phillips Brooks to write "O Little Town of Bethlehem". What year did he visit?
30. The author and composer of "Toyland" helped found what publishing organization?
31. Which song did Eddie Cantor help make popular?
32. Which song was written by a Russian emigrant?
33. Which song debuted in the film "Meet Me In St.Louis"?
34. Which three Christmas songs did Gene Autry help make famous?
35. Mel Torme composed the music for which song?
36. Eddy Arnold composed the music for which song?
37. What comedian helped debut "Silver Bells" in the movie "The Lemon Drop Kid" in 1950?
38. Who earned the title "Father of American Church and Public School Music"?
39. Which American Christmas song composer studied music with Felix Mendelssohn in Europe?
40. Which song is sung to a Swedish tune from 1582?

41. Which composer was related to American financier J.P. Morgan?
42. Which composer wrote the Auburn University football march?
43. Who played flute in the John Philip Sousa Band?
44. Which songwriting team wrote the Easter song Peter Cottontail"?
45. Which Christmas song had the words added two years after the music was composed?
46. Who created "Rudolph, The Red-Nosed Reindeer"?
47. Which Christmas song did Judy Garland help popularize?
48. What does "wassail" mean?
49. Who put together the first modern collection of Christmas songs in 1823?
50. Which popular 19th century Christmas song is totally anonymous in it's creation?
51. Which Christmas song was re-titled in 1958?
52. Who founded the St. Nicholas Music Publishing Company?
53. Which two songs were inspired by ringing church bells?
54. Which song did the Fisk Univ. Jubilee Singers popularize?
55. Which song is sometimes known as "Winchester Old"?
56. Which song is based on a legend about the Duke of Bohemia?
57. Which 1871 carol collection by John Stainer did much to promote carols of all types?
58. Which song debuted at a midnight mass on Christmas Eve 1847?
59. In which song do the words "Gloria In Excelsis Deo" appear?
60. What famous tune is used with "What Child Is This?"
61. What year was Silent Night first heard in America?
62. Mykola Leontovych was what nationality?
63. Which song took 120 years to finalize in its current form?
64. Which two songs were set to music within 24 hours of their first performance?
65. Which Christmas melody did Wolfgang Mozart use for a piano and violin duet in the mid-eighteenth century?
66. Which carol has also been called "The Portuguese Hymn"?
67. Which song was initially denounced for its "lack of musical taste"?
68. Which hymn was originally called "A Hymn For Christmas Day"?
69. Which composer became a naturalized English citizen in 1727?
70. Which song took 165 years to finalize in its current form?
71. What was a "broadside"?
72. Who is the Christmas tune "St. Louis" named after?
73. Which composer was knighted in 1888?
74. Which hymn is also known as "The Childrens Carol"?
75. What other Christmas song did Phillips Brooks and Lewis Redner create?
76. Which carol originated with the "Yule" celebrations?
77. Which hymn is called "Westminster Carol" in England?
78. Passages from Luke where the angels sing "Glory to God in the Highest, And on earth, peace to men of good will" are referred to as?
79. Who is often mistaken as being the author of many Christmashymns, because he arranged so many?
80. What Christmas hymn did Martin Luther write in 1535?

Christmas Music Trivia Answers

1. St. Francis of Assisi
2. Middle Ages
3. Nahum Tate
4. The Holly & The Ivy
5. Charles Wesley
6. While Shepherds Watched Their Flocks
7. Isaac Watts
8. Phillips Brooks
9. Adeste Fidelis
10. From Christmas to Epiphany
11. A Visit From St. Nicholas
12. God Rest Ye Merry Gentlemen
13. Stille Nacht
14. Henry Wadsworth Longfellow
15. Away In A Manger
16. The Messiah
17. Henry Smart
18. Give Gifts Each Day
19. Waits
20. Christmas Eve
21. Germany
22. Father Of Modern English Hymnody
23. It Came Upon The Midnight Clear
24. English
25. Advent
26. Epiphany
27. Christmas
28. O Holy Night,
    Angels We Have Heard On High
29. 1865
30. ASCAP
31. Santa Claus Is Coming To Town
32. White Christmas
33. Have Yourself A Merry Little Christmas
34. Here Comes Santa Claus,
    Rudolph, The Red-Nosed Reindeer
    Frosty The Snowman
35. The Christmas Song
36. C-H-R-I-S-T-M-A-S
37. Bob Hope
38. Lowell Mason
39. Richard Storrs Willis
40. Good King Wencelas
41. James S. Pierpont
42. Robert Allen
43. Meredith Willson
44. Jack Rollins/Steve Nelson
45. Sleigh Ride
46. Robert May
47. Have Yourself A Merry Little Christmas
48. A Song To Wish Good Health
49. Davies Gilbert
50. Jolly Old St. Nicholas
51. Carol Of The Drum
52. Johnny Marks
53. Hark! The Herald Angels Sing,
    I Heard The Bells On Christmas Day
54. Go Tell It On The Mountain
55. While Shepherds Watched Their Flocks
56. Good King Wencelas
57. Christmas Carols, New & Old
58. O Holy Night
59. Angels From The Realms Of Glory
60. Greensleeves
61. 1839
62. Ukrainian
63. Joy To The World
64. Silent Night, O Little Town Of Bethlehem
65. The Melody For Deck The Halls
66. O Come All Ye Faithful
67. O Holy Night
68. Hark! The Herald Angels Sing
69. George F. Handel
70. While Shepherds Watched Their Flocks
71. A Sheet Of Paper That Carols Were Printed On
72. Lewis Redner
73. John Stainer
74. Away In A Manger
75. Everywhere, Everywhere, Christmas Tonight
76. Deck The Halls
77. Angels We Have Heard On High
78. The Angels Hymn
79. John Stainer
80. From Heaven Above

Index Of Authors, Arrangers, Composers & Translators
(Including Their Primary Occupations)

Adam, Adolphe Charles [Composer]	(7/24, 1803-5/3, 1856)	O Holy Night
Allen, Robert [Composer]	(2/5, 1927-)	The Christmas Song
Anderson, Leroy [Composer]	(6/29, 1908-5/18, 1975)	Sleigh Ride
Anschutz, Ernst Gebhard [Poet]	(1800-1861)	O Christmas Tree
Arnold, Eddy [Singer]	(5/15, 1918-)	Christmas
Autry, Gene Orvon [Singer, Actor, Businessman]	(9/29, 1907-10/2, 1998)	Here Comes Santa Claus
Berlin, Irving [Composer]	(5/11, 1888-9/22, 1989)	White Christmas
Bernard, Felix [Musician]	(4/28, 1897-10/20, 1944)	Winter Wonderland
Blane, Ralph [Composer]	(7/26, 1914-11/13, 1995)	Have A Merry Christmas
Brooks, Phillips [Episcopal Clergyman]	(12/13, 1835-1/23, 1893)	O Little Town of Bethlehem
Burnap, Uzziah C. [Dry Goods Merchant/Musician]	(6/17, 1834-12/8, 1900)	It Came Upon The Midnight
Cahn, Sammy [Music Publisher]	(6/18, 1913-1/15, 1993)	Let It Snow, Let It Snow
Calkin, John Baptiste [Organist]	(3/16, 1827-5/15, 1905)	I Heard The Bells
Cappeau, Placide [Wine Commissionaire/Poet]	(1808-1877)	O Holy Night
Carson, Jenny Lou [Songwriter]	(1915-1978)	Christmas
Coffin, Henry Sloane [Presbyterian Clergyman]	(1/5, 1877-11/25, 1954)	O Come, O Come Emmanuel
Coots, John Frederick [Composer/Songwriter]	(5/2, 1897-4/8, 1985)	Santa Is Coming To Town
Cummings, William H. [Music Teacher]	(8/22, 1831-6/6, 1915)	Hark! The Herald Angels
Davis, Katherine K. [Music Teacher/Composer]	(6/25, 1892-4/20, 1980)	The Little Drummer Boy
Dix, William C. [Insurance Agent/Poet]	(6/14, 1837-9/9, 1898)	What Child Is This?
Dwight, John Sullivan [Unitarian Clergyman]	(5/13, 1813-9/5, 1893)	O Holy Night

Evans, Ray Bernard [Musician/Songwriter]	(2/4, 1915-)	Silver Bells
Gannon, James Kimball [Lawyer/Songwriter]	(11/18, 1900-4/29, 1974)	I'll Be Home For Christmas
Gillespie, Haven [Journeyman Printer/Songwriter]	(2/6, 1888-3/14, 1975)	Santa Is Coming To Town
Gruber, Franz Xaver [School Teacher]	(11/25, 1787-6/7, 1863)	Silent Night
Haldeman, Oakley [Composer/Publisher]	(7/17, 109-1986)	Here Comes Santa Claus
Hanby, Benjamin R. [Songwriter/Compiler]	(7/22, 1833-3/16, 1867)	Up On The Housetop
Handel, George F. [Composer]	(2/23, 1685-4/14, 1759)	While Shepherds Watched
Harrington, Karl P. [Latin Professor/Music Scholar]	(6/13, 1861-11/14, 1953)	There's A Song In The Air
Hayes, Billy [Musician/Singer]	(2/17, 1906-)	Blue Christmas
Helmore, Thomas [Congregational Clergyman/English Teacher]	(5/7, 1811-7/6, 1890)	O Come, O Come Emmanuel
Herbert, Victor [Composer]	(2/1, 1859-5/25, 1924)	Toyland
Hohman, Minna Louise [Songwriter]	( )	Ring Christmas Bells
Holland, Josiah Gilbert [Newspaper/Magazine Editor]	(7/24, 1819-10/12, 1881)	There's A Song In The Air
Hopkins Jr., John Henry [Episcopal Clergyman]	(10/28, 1820-8/14, 1891)	We Three Kings
Johnson, Jay W. [Music Performer/Songwriter]	(3/23, 1903-1986)	Blue Christmas
Kent, Walter [Architect/Musician]	(11/29, 1911-3/1, 1994)	I'll Be Home For Christmas
Leontovych, Mykola D. [Composer]	(12/1, 1877-1/23, 1921)	Ring Christmas Bells
Livingston, Jay Harold [Musician/Songwriter]	(3/28, 1915-)	Silver Bells
Longfellow, Henry W. [Modern Language Professor/Poet]	(2/27, 1807-3/24, 1882)	I Heard The Bells
MacDonough, Glen [Lyricist]	(11/12, 1870-3/30, 1924)	Toyland
MacGimsey, Robert [Lawyer/Whistler]	(1898-3/13, 1979)	Sweet Little Jesus Boy
Marks, Johnny D. [Music Publisher/Musician]	(11/10, 1909-9/3, 1985)	Rudolph The Red Nosed Deer
Martin, Hugh [Composer]	(8/11, 1914-)	Have A Merry Christmas

Mason, Lowell [Music Teacher/Composer]	(1/8, 1792-8/11, 1872)	Joy To The World
McFarland, John Thomas [Methodist Clergyman/Educator]	(1/2, 1851-12/22, 1913)	Away In A Manger
Mendelssohn, Felix [Composer]	(2/3, 1809-11/4, 1847)	Hark! The Herald Angels
Mohr, Joseph [Roman Catholic Priest]	(12/11, 1792-12/5, 1848)	Silent Night
Montgomery, James [Newspaper Publisher/Editor]	(11/4, 1771-4/30, 1854)	Angels From The Realms
Murray, James Ramsey [Music Editor]	(3/7, 1841-3/10, 1905)	Away In A Manger
Neale, John Mason [Clergyman/Translator]	(1/24, 1818-8/6, 1866)	Good King Wencelas
Nelson, Steve Edward [Composer]	(11/24, 1907-1981)	Frosty The Snowman
Niles, John Jacob [Folk Music Collector/Singer/Composer]	(4/28, 1892-3/1, 1980)	I Wonder As I Wander
Oakeley, Frederick [Roman Catholic Clergyman]	(9/5, 1802-1/29, 1880)	O Come All Ye Faithful
Onorati, Henry V. [Music Executive]	(1/25, 1912-1993)	The Little Drummer Boy
Parish, Mitchell [Lyricist]	(7/10, 1900-4/10, 1993)	Sleigh Ride
Pierpont, James S. [Composer]	(1822-1893)	Jingle Bells
Redner, Lewis Henry [Real Estate Broker]	(12/15, 1830-8/29, 1908)	O Little Town Of Bethlehem
Rollins, Walter E. [Lyricist]	(9/15, 1906-1/1, 1973)	Frosty The Snowman
Sears, Edmund Hamilton [Unitarian Clergyman]	(4/6, 1810-1/14, 1876)	It Came Upon The Midnight
Simeone, Harry [Choral Conductor]	(5/9, 1911-)	The Little Drummer Boy
Smart, Henry Thomas [Organist]	(10/26, 1813-7/6, 1879)	Angels From The Realms
Smith, Richard D. [Newspaper Editor]	(9/29, 1901-9/28, 1935)	Winter Wonderland
Stainer, John [Music Composer/Editor/Teacher]	(6/13, 1840-3/31, 1901)	What Child Is This?
Stillman, Al [Music Hall Staffmember/Songwriter]	(6/26, 1906-2/17, 1979)	Home For The Holidays
Styne, Jule [Music Publisher/Composer/Producer]	(12/31, 1905-9/20, 1994)	Let It Snow, Let It Snow
Tate, Nahum [Poet/Playwright]	(1652-8/12, 1715)	While Shepherds Watched

Torme, Mel [Singer/Entertainer]	(9/13, 1925-6/5, 1999)	The Christmas Song
Wade, John Francis [Music Teacher/Writer]	(1711-8/16, 1786)	O Come All Ye Faithful
Watts, Isaac [Hymnwriter]	(7/17, 1674-11/25, 1748)	Joy To The World
Wells, Robert [Musician]	(1922-)	The Christmas Song
Wesley, Charles [Methodist Clergyman/Hymnwriter]	(12/28, 1707-3/29, 1788)	Hark! The Herald Angels
Whitefield, George [Anglican Clergyman]	(12/16, 1714-9/30, 1770)	Hark! The Herald Angels
Wilhousky, Peter J. [Music Composer/Conductor]	(1902-1978)	Ring Christmas Bells
Willis, Richard Storrs [Music Critic/Editor]	(2/10, 1819-5/7, 1900)	It Came Upon The Midnight
Willson, Meredith [Composer]	(5/18, 1902-6/17, 1984)	It's Beginning To Look
Work, Frederick Jerome [Composer]	(1880-1/24, 1942)	Go Tell It On The Mountain
Work, John Wesley [Music Teacher]	(8/6, 1872-9/7, 1925)	Go Tell It On The Mountain
Young, John Freeman [Episcopal Clergyman]	(10/30, 1820-11/15, 1885)	Silent Night

Joy to the world! the Lord is come,
  Let earth receive her King
Let every heart prepare him room
  And heaven and nature sing

Joy to the world! the Savior reigns,
  Let men their songs employ
While hills and floods, rocks, hills and plains
  Repeat the sounding joy